P9-DHT-793

flea
market
make-
overs

flea market make-overs

25 projects for fabulous home furnishings

by bj berti

clarkson potter/publishers **new york**

Copyright © 2000 by B. J. Berti
Photographs copyright © 2000 by George Ross

Photographs on pages 13 and 14 © 2000 by Vincent Scilla

All rights reserved. No part of this book may be reproduced or transmitted in any form or by any means, electronic or mechanical, including photocopying, recording, or by any information storage and retrieval system, without permission in writing from the publisher.

Published by Clarkson Potter/Publishers, New York, New York.
Member of the Crown Publishing Group.

Random House, Inc. New York, Toronto, London, Sydney, Auckland
www.randomhouse.com

CLARKSON N. POTTER is a trademark and POTTER and colophon are registered trademarks of Random House, Inc.

Printed in the United States of America

Design by Lauren Monchik

Library of Congress Cataloging-in-Publication Data
Berti, BJ
Flea market makeovers : 25 projects for fabulous home furnishings / by BJ Berti.—1st ed.
p. cm.
1. Furniture—Repairing—Amateurs' manuals. 2. Used furniture.
I. Title.
TT199 .B475 2000
684.1'0028'8—dc21

99-086294

ISBN 0-609-60491-0

10 9 8 7 6 5 4 3 2 1

First Edition

f o r   v i n c e

without him it would have been impossible

acknowledgments

Many, many thanks go to: Denise McGann and Les Pockell for their encouragement and support. Pam Krauss and Chloe Smith for their editorial expertise and guidance. George Ross for his keen eye, attention to detail, and great patience. Lauren Monchik for her creative hand. Maryellen Stadtlander for her always cheerful and helpful presence. Yvonne Beecher and Stuart Klein for being there when I needed them.

Also thanks to my mother, Elaine, for conveying to me her love and appreciation of fine design, and to my father, David, for including me on all those Saturday excursions to the local thrift stores.

And last but not least a special thanks to my son, Alex, for all his help and patience.

contents

There is no such thing as a

"worthless piece of junk."

Even the most humble castoff, with some imagination, loving care, and elbow grease, can be transformed into a practical and stylish piece for your home.

With the rise in popularity of the "shabby chic" look and a more eclectic, personalized approach to decorating, more and more of us are looking for unique pieces, perhaps with a bit of patina or the warmth of old wood, to lend distinction to our homes. And older pieces often boast better materials and construction than brand-new pieces costing many times more. But while it is easy to spot the good stuff and pay the price for it at fancy antique shops, you have to look a bit harder to find the hidden treasures at more palatable prices. Fortunately, a lot of neat stuff gets overlooked at thrift shops, flea markets, yard sales, and country auctions. These are the pieces that are basically attractive but might be painted an ugly color or need recovering—or maybe just a good cleaning! Start to look at the solidly made but otherwise imperfect pieces that find no takers and you may uncover diamonds in the rough more readily than you imagine. They are out there. I know because I am always finding them and you can too.

Do keep in mind that not every piece is worth salvaging; some may truly be beyond redemption or simply require more

work than would be justified by the end result. Here are a few helpful rules I use when sorting through the offerings at my local thrift shop:

- If it's cheap enough and I can imagine how it might look once I've painted it or recovered it, I buy it, even if I don't have a specific place or need for it at the time. Sometimes I have a piece for years before I can figure out the perfect use for it.
- Pay attention to the object's overall shape and design; I won't buy something unless its shape is pleasing to me.
- Ignore the current color or fabric; if it has good bones it can usually be made to look good again.
- After you think you are finished looking, look again—some of the best things I've acquired were things I'd overlooked at first.
- Don't buy something that's really falling apart—unless it's

a *real* bargain. In that case, take a chance. You can always throw it out or send it back to the thrift store.

Certain things are always worth buying assuming the price is right: glass or ceramic lamp bases, especially those from the thirties and forties; wooden picture frames; stools and benches (old piano benches can frequently be found in thrift shops); wooden chairs with interesting shapes. Individual kitchen chairs that were originally sold as a set with a table can frequently be found at very reasonable prices. Small, odd wood tables always come in handy and wooden bookcases are easily transformed into elegant and practical storage. Small hanging shelves are also useful pieces to have, and keep an eye out for pairs of just about anything, which look especially nice once they've been restored.

Take some time to educate your eye to recognize good design. Look at design and art books and shelter magazines, browse the higher price antique stores and shows, and frequent home design shops. Seek out museums with good design collections and learn from friends whose style you admire. Once you have a solid foundation, learn to trust your instincts and work to develop your style. Be inspired by the things that you love, experiment with color and pattern, and work toward a sensibility and a look that is truly your own.

It is fun to combine styles, and in today's pared-down interiors the older, simpler pieces you have created out of junk can make strong, clear statements. Integrate your revitalized, humble pieces with newer, finer things and each will look the better for it.

lamps and shades

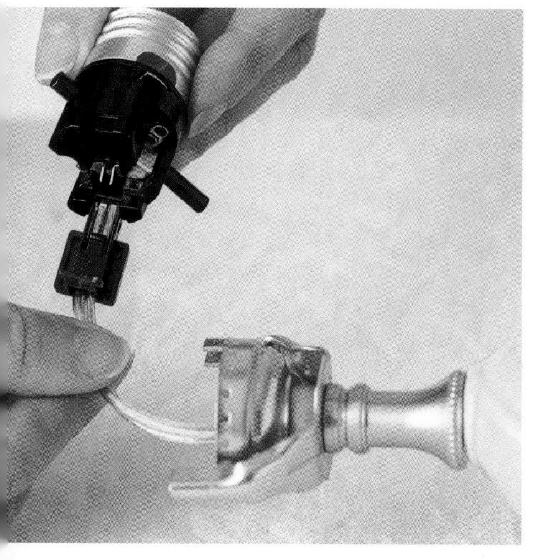

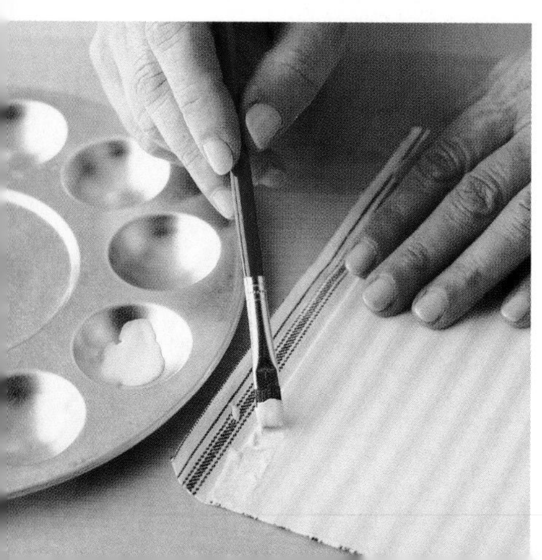

lighting is one of the most

important elements in a home, and for me, it really determines how comfortable I feel. The right balance between light and shadow is a key element in any room—think about how bright overhead lights make you feel alert in an office setting and then picture yourself reading in a cozy chair in the warmly lit corner of your living room. Lighting is also one of the easiest and fastest ways to transform a space. Finding distinctive lamps or creating them from interesting architectural elements you unearth at flea markets or elsewhere requires only minimal effort. The end result is lamps that are both unique and affordable.

I found wiring a lamp very intimidating at first, but after a few attempts, I discovered how easy it really is. (If the thought of working with electrical wiring makes you nervous, just remember a lamp wire does not have electricity running through it until it's plugged into an outlet.) Using the newer quick-wiring or self-clamping socket fixtures, which don't require you to strip wires or wrap them around the terminals, makes the whole process even simpler. You can also buy prewired plugs.

Finding the right shade for a lamp is a little more challenging, but it's the most creative part of the process. The only real way to tell which shade best fits the lamp is by actually seeing how the shade will look on the base. Always take the lamp base with you when you go to pick out the shade, and try as many different shades as possible. You'll know instinctively when you've hit the right combination—they'll just look right together.

However, there are a few basic concepts to keep in mind when shopping for a lamp shade:

- Certain shapes work better on certain bases. Cone-shaped shades complement bases that are wider at the bottom; bell-shaped shades look best with vase- and urn-shaped bases; oval, square, and rectangular shades are good matches for correspondingly shaped bases.
- The bottom of the lamp shade should float just above the top of the lamp base. A frequent mistake is choosing a lamp shade that is too big for the lamp; if you are torn between two, go with the smaller-scale one. The harp (the metal bracket that supports the shade), if there is one, is easily removable and can be replaced if it's too tall (or short) to accommodate the shade you pick.
- If you are finding it difficult to choose, remember that in terms of materials, a simple paper shade is frequently the most appropriate choice.

Once you get a feel for pairing lamp shades and bases you might like to try to make your own shades. If a lamp's existing shade looks in balance with the base but is not the right material or color, use it as the starting point for the new shade. But if you are starting with nothing, you'll first need to figure out the best shape and proportions for the new lamp shade. Follow the guidelines above, or experiment with lamp shades around your home. Decorating magazines can also serve as a fast source for inspiration. All of these exercises should give you a good idea of the shape of the lamp shade you're looking for.

Once I decide on the shape for my new shade, I make a rough scale drawing of the base and shade on graph paper to check that the proportions work with each other. Don't be afraid to experiment a little until you are satisfied with the overall look; buy extra sets of rings (these determine the top and bottom circumference of the shade) in different sizes if you still aren't sure—they are a minimal investment for a wonderful handmade shade that will shed a lovely light for a long time.

20,000 LEAGUES UNDER THE SEA
JULES VERNE

Distressed Column Lamps

THESE MINIATURE CORINTHIAN COLUMNS HAD ACQUIRED THREE DIFFERENT LAYERS OF PAINT BY THE TIME THEY CAME INTO MY HANDS. ORIGINALLY PAINTED A DARK TAN, AT SOME POINT THEY HAD ALSO BEEN PAINTED WHITE AND THEN BLUE-GREEN. THE COLUMNS WERE NICELY DISTRESSED, WITH SOME OF THE ORIGINAL WOOD SHOWING THROUGH THE LAYERS OF ARTFULLY PEELING PAINT, ALMOST AS THOUGH THEY HAD SPRUNG FROM SOME ANCIENT RUIN. TO THIS DAY, I HAVE NO IDEA WHAT THEIR ORIGINAL PURPOSE WAS, BUT I DECIDED THEY WOULD MAKE GREAT LAMPS.

INITIALLY, THEIR HEIGHT WAS A DRAWBACK. IT TOOK ME A WHILE TO FIND SOMEONE WITH THE RIGHT LENGTH DRILL TO MAKE THE OPENING FOR THE THREADED ROD THAT EXTENDS THROUGH THE LAMP AND TO FIGURE OUT HOW THE BASE SHOULD BE CONSTRUCTED. I'M REALLY PLEASED WITH HOW I TRANSFORMED THE COLUMNS IN THE END. YOU CAN USE THIS TECHNIQUE WITH ANY COLUMN OR PIECE OF TURNED WOOD, SUCH AS A BANISTER OR TABLE LEG. EVEN NEW ONES COULD WORK: THEY CAN BE PAINTED LIKE THE BASES TO LOOK OLD.

materials

Wooden columns
4 basswood rosettes (2 small and 2 large)
Wood glue
Concentrated artist's acrylic in raw umber, raw sienna, aqua, green umber, titanium white (or colors of choice)
Plastic dishes
Small artist's brush or sea sponge
Glaze medium
Drill
Pliers
Wire cutter

FOR EACH LAMP
1 threaded rod/hex nut/lock washer/check ring/bushing
2 vase caps (1 large and 1 small)
1 threaded brass neck
1 harp/harp bottom
1 lamp socket with three-way switch
1 cord set with attached plug
Pressure-sensitive felt
1 lamp shade
1 lamp finial

1 MAKE A BASE FOR THE COLUMN BY CENTERING THE smaller wood rosette on top of the larger one. Glue them together with wood glue. Set them aside until the glue is dry. [photo A]

2 SQUEEZE A SMALL AMOUNT OF RAW UMBER AND RAW sienna paint into a plastic dish. Use the sponge to dab both shades of paint separately onto the base, completely covering the surface in an irregular, mottled fashion. Let it dry.

3 ON ANOTHER PLATE, SQUEEZE A SMALL AMOUNT EACH OF the aqua and green umber paint; mix each with a small amount of white paint and glaze medium to make two shades of light and dark aqua. Use the sponge to dab the two shades of paint onto the base, mottling irregularly. Let some of the under color show through. Let it dry. Apply another coat of mottled aqua paint if needed. Let it dry. (If you're starting from scratch with new columns, they can be painted in the same way, following all the steps above.) [photo B]

4 DRILL OR HAVE A HOLE DRILLED THROUGH EACH COLUMN and the centers of the stacked bases wide enough to accommodate the threaded rod. On the underside of each base, using a 1⅛-inch drill bit, drill out the center hole three fourths of the way through the base. This will widen the center hole to accommodate the washer and nut that will hold the threaded rod in place.

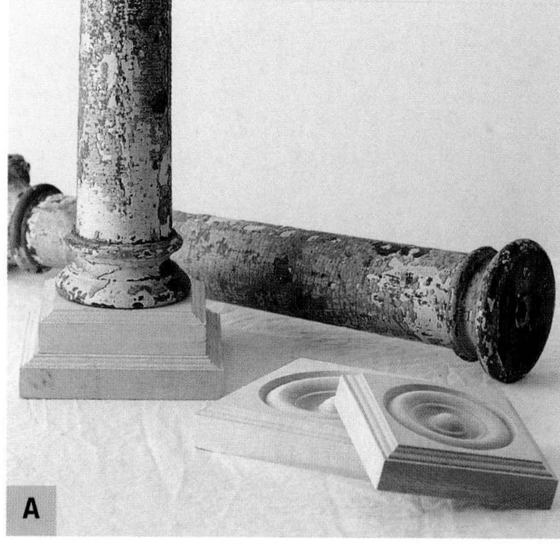
A

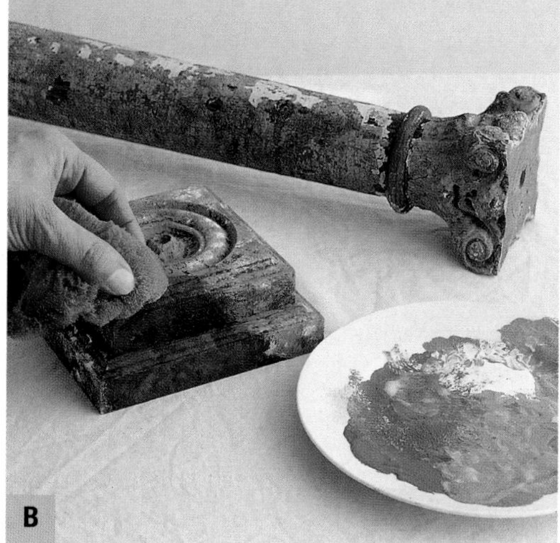
B

C

D

5 DRILL ANOTHER HOLE THROUGH THE SIDE OF THE bottom section of the base parallel to the bottom edge of the base and centered from side to side and from top to bottom, all the way through the base, ending where it meets the vertical hole. The electrical cord will exit here, allowing the base to rest securely on a table.

6 SLIP THE CHECK RING ONTO THE THREADED ROD, then tighten with a lock washer and nut. Screw the bushing onto the bottom of the rod. Place the columns on the rosettes with the threaded rod extending up through both. This will help hold the column and base in place while the rest of the lamp is being assembled. [photo C]

7 USE THE PLIERS TO PULL THE THREADED ROD UP through the columns and stack the two vase caps on the rod with the larger one on the bottom. Screw the brass neck onto the rod. Add the harp bottom and screw the socket base onto the threaded rod, tightening the socket base set screw. [photo D]

making bases

If you preferred, you could make, or have someone make for you, the base for the lamp out of a piece of hardwood. I was lucky to find these rosettes in two graduated sizes that worked with the diameter of the column to use as the base for the lamp. Look for them at a lumberyard or a store like Home Depot or Lowe's. They are part of the moldings that go into framing a door. I used rosettes made from basswood, but if I were doing it again I would probably choose hardwood, which costs more but is a little easier to work with. When working with the basswood, the drilling has to be done with care because though the wood is soft, it has a tendency to shred if you are not cautious.

8 INSERT THE LAMP CORD THROUGH THE HOLE IN THE SIDE of the base and then up through the threaded rod and out the socket base. If the cord sticks going through the wood base, rub a little petroleum jelly on the outside covering of the cord, not on the end. Pull out some extra wire at the top so you have plenty to work with.

9 SPLIT THE WIRE AND MAKE AN UNDERWRITER'S KNOT IF there is room in the cap. Strip the ends of each wire, exposing ½ inch of bare copper strands. Twist the strands of each wire tightly together, then wrap the neutral wire (covered with ridged insulation) clockwise around the silver terminal screw, tightening the screw securely over the loop. Wrap the smoother hot wire clockwise around the brass terminal and tighten. Snap the socket body in place and replace the insulating cardboard sleeve and the shell.

10 PRESS OR GLUE A PRECUT PIECE OF PRESSURE-SENSITIVE felt to the bottom of the lamp. Attach the harp, place the lamp shade on top, and screw in the finial.

Green Lamp

I FOUND THIS BASE AT A THRIFT STORE, HIDDEN AMONG THE DISHES AND CHINA AND LOOKING VERY DIRTY. I WAS ATTRACTED FIRST TO THE COLOR AND THEN TO THE UNUSUAL SHAPE, BUT BECAUSE THE BASE WAS MISSING ALL THE HARDWARE AS WELL AS THE CORD AND PLUG, I WASN'T QUITE SURE WHAT IT WAS. AFTER LOOKING AT IT AWHILE I FIGURED OUT THAT IT WAS INDEED A LAMP BASE MISSING ALL ITS PARTS. AFTER I INVESTED A MODEST SUM IN ELECTRICAL PARTS AND FABRICATED A JAUNTY NEW SHADE, IT WAS BACK IN BUSINESS AND BETTER THAN EVER.

YOU CAN USE THE TECHNIQUE SHOWN ON THE PAGES THAT FOLLOW TO TURN ANY HOLLOW OBJECT INTO A LAMP.

materials

- Ceramic lamp base
- Threaded rod/hex nut/lock washer/check ring/bushing
- Pliers
- Threaded brass neck
- Cord set with attached plug
- Harp/harp bottom
- Quick-wiring lamp socket with push switch
- Wire cutter
- Pressure-sensitive felt
- Lamp finial

1 SLIP THE CHECK RING ONTO THE bottom of the threaded rod, then tighten with a lock washer and nut. Screw the bushing onto the bottom of the rod. Place the threaded rod in the opening in the base, inserting it from underneath. Screw the brass neck onto the rod. Insert the end of the cord through the hole in the side of the base and then out through the top. [photo A]

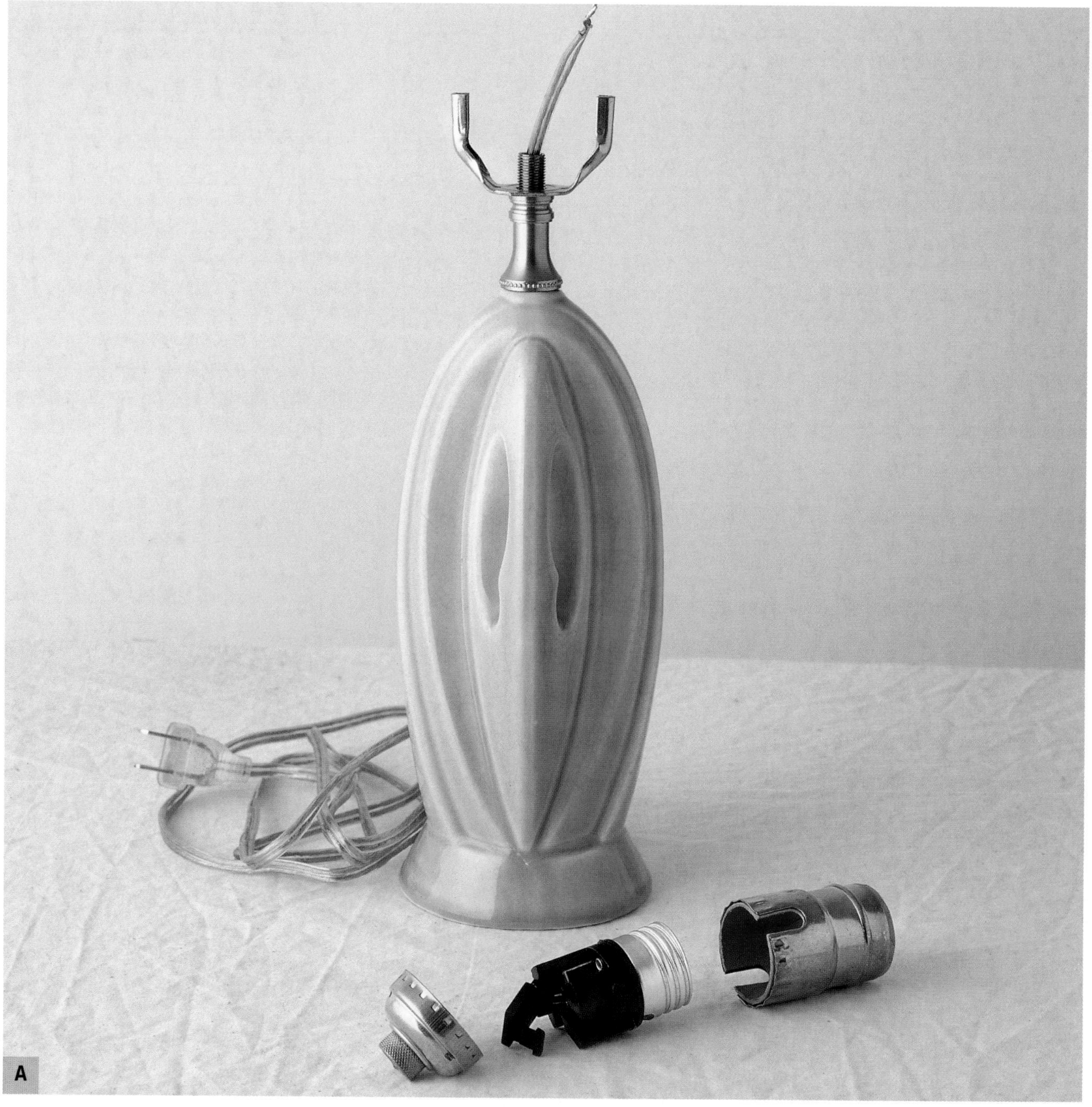

A

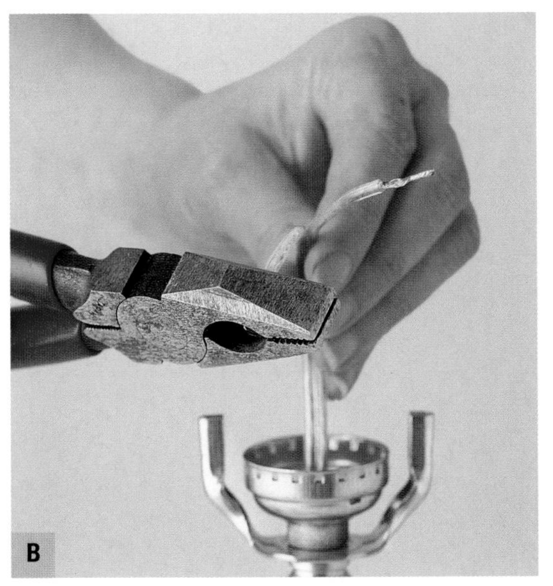
B

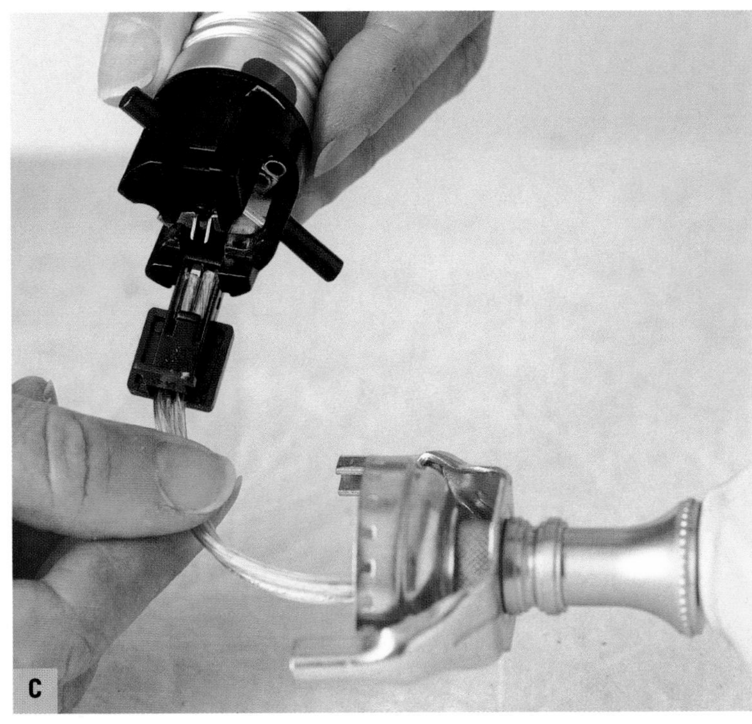
C

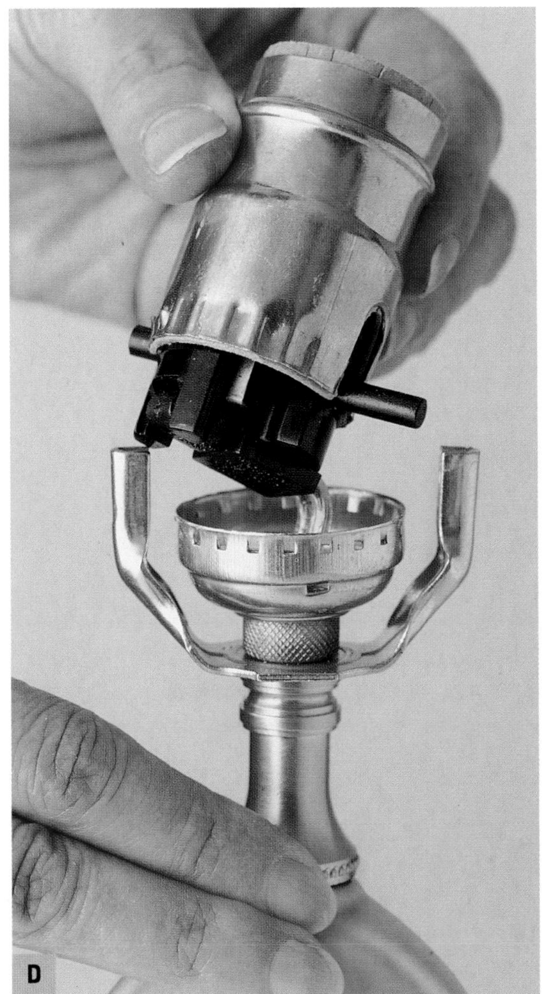
D

2 ADD THE HARP BOTTOM AND SCREW THE SOCKET BASE onto the threaded rod, tightening the socket base set screw. Pull out some extra wire at the top so you have plenty to work with. [photo B]

3 IF YOU ARE USING A QUICK-CONNECT SOCKET (SELF-clamping socket), as shown here, cut the end of the wire straight across so it's flush with the covering. Push the wire firmly into the slots as far as it will go and snap shut. The insulation does not need to be stripped from cords inserted into a self-clamping socket. [photo C]

4 SNAP THE SOCKET BODY IN PLACE AND REPLACE THE insulating cardboard sleeve and the shell. [photo D]

5 PRESS OR GLUE A PRECUT PIECE OF PRESSURE-SENSITIVE felt to the bottom of the lamp. Attach the harp, place the lamp shade on top, and screw in the finial.

Woven Paper Drum Shade

THE WOVEN PAPER LAMP SHADE CAN BE MADE FROM ANY HEAT-RESISTANT, HEAVY CARD STOCK. I CHOSE A HEAVY, SMOOTH-SURFACED PRINTMAKING PAPER; BUT YOU WILL FIND A VARIED SELECTION OF SUITABLE PAPERS AT MOST ART SUPPLY STORES. A CYLINDRICAL SHADE LIKE THIS IS PROPERLY CALLED A DRUM SHADE. IT WORKS VERY WELL WITH BASES THAT HAVE A CLEAN, VERTICAL SHAPE.

materials

- 1 set of bottom and top lamp shade rings (with washer top fitting) of equal size
- Large sheet of heat-resistant, heavy card stock
- Soft lead pencil
- Clear plastic ruler
- Craft knife
- Metal-edged ruler
- Cutting mat
- Masking tape
- Square-tipped artist's brush
- Craft glue
- Soft white eraser
- Clothespins
- Wax paper
- Small weights
- Double-fold bias tape to match card stock
- Compass
- Scissors

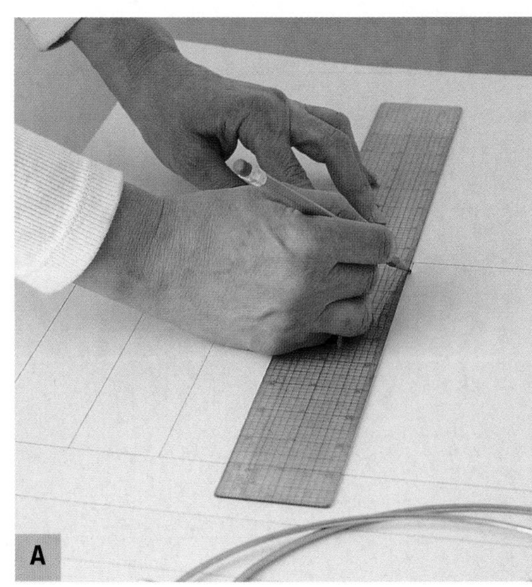

A

1 MEASURE THE CIRCUMFERENCE OF THE RINGS AND ADD 1 inch. Use this measurement to draw a rectangle on the card stock, with short sides corresponding to the height you want your lamp shade to be. Draw a second rectangle with the same dimensions above it on the card stock.

2 TO MAKE THE HORIZONTAL STRIPS, WITH THE PLASTIC ruler and pencil, lightly draw lines parallel to one rectangle's length at 1½-inch increments. You may need to adjust the measurements to fit your paper's dimensions, making sure to divide the paper into an odd number of strips. (Be sure the strips are at least 1 inch wide.)

B

3 TO MAKE THE VERTICAL STRIPS, WITH THE PLASTIC RULER and pencil, lightly draw lines parallel to the other rectangle's width at 1½-inch increments. Adjust the measurements so the strips are the exact same width as the long strips above. [photo A]

4 WITH THE CRAFT KNIFE AND THE METAL-EDGED RULER, cut out the 2 rectangles. Cut each into strips, cutting along the pencil lines. [photo B]

C

5 ALIGN THE VERTICAL STRIPS WITH THE LONG EDGES parallel and touching on the cutting mat. Use the masking tape to secure the ends of the strips to the mat on one short side only. Weave the horizontal strips under and over the vertical ones, pushing them as tightly against each of the previous strips as possible until they are all used. Remove the tape. [photo C]

D

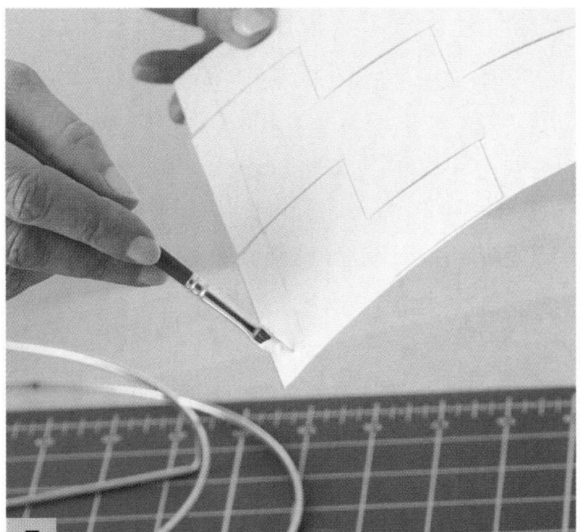

F

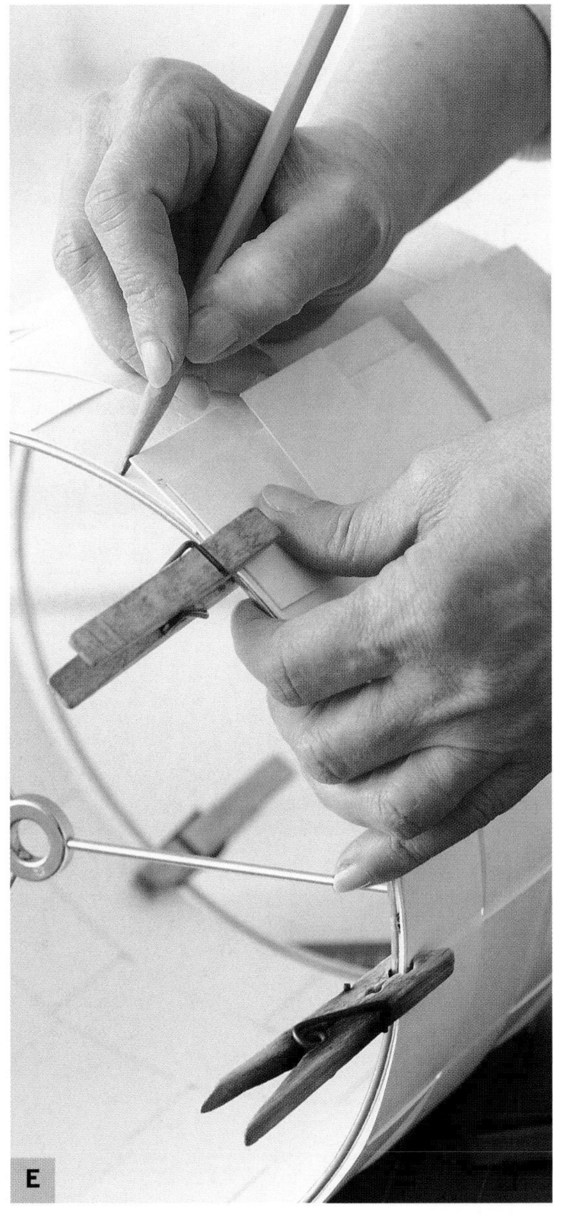

E

6 WITH THE SMALL BRUSH, APPLY GLUE TO THE ENDS OF THE strips where they overlap all along the outside edges. Press together and let dry for an hour. Turn the woven paper rectangle over and repeat on the other side. Again, let dry completely before proceeding. Erase any pencil marks left on the card stock. [photo D]

7 HOLD THE BOTTOM (SPOKELESS) RING IN ONE HAND. PLACE the bottom center front of the woven paper rectangle on the wire ring and clamp the edge to the ring with a clothespin. Following the natural curve of the paper, fit the shade around the ring, fastening it as you go with the clothespins. Work first toward the left until you reach the outside edge. Return to the center front and fit the right half of the shade to the ring. Repeat for the top ring. Adjust the fit so the top and bottom of the shade fit evenly around the edge of the rings and there are no gaps: There will be approximately a ½-inch overlap where the back seam edges meet. With the back seam facing you, lightly mark the top and bottom seam overlap. [photo E]

8 REMOVE THE CLOTHESPINS AND SET THE RINGS ASIDE. Place the shade on the cutting mat with the right side faceup. Use the straightedge if necessary to trim the overlap to ½ inch. Turn the shade over and with the wrong side faceup apply a thin, even coat of glue along the entire length of the back seam overlap, keeping within the imaginary line indicating the inside edge of the seam allowance. Lifting the edge of the shade, hold it so the right side is facing you and apply a thin, even coat along the entire length of the seam allowance on the outside (right side). [photo F]

9 BENDING THE SHADE INTO SHAPE, LINE UP THE TOP EDGE along the pencil mark and fasten with a clothespin. Secure the bottom edge in the same fashion. Hold the glued seam together for a few minutes until the glue sets, then place, seam-side down, on a piece of wax paper. Remove the clothespins and place small weights along the back seam. Let dry for 15 to 20 minutes, removing the weights when the glue is completely dry.

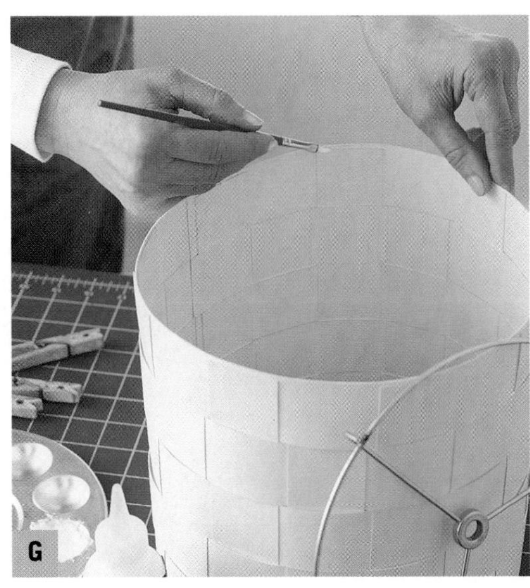
G

10 STAND THE SHADE ON THE WORK SURFACE WITH THE TOP resting on the table. With the brush, apply a thin line of glue along the bottom inside edge of the shade, rotating the shade as you work. Ease the bottom ring into place starting at the center front, positioning the weld in the ring slightly to the right of the back seam. Fasten the ring in place with the clothespins, making sure the ring is positioned evenly inside the shade. Repeat with the top ring, positioning one of the top ring's 3 spokes in line with the back seam of the shade. Let the glue dry for 20 minutes and then remove the clothespins. [photo G]

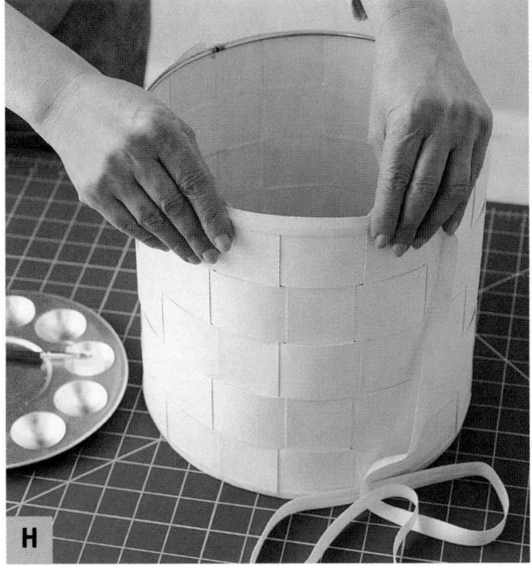
H

11 TO BIND THE TOP AND BOTTOM EDGES OF THE SHADE TO THE wire rings, use a trim such as double-fold bias tape. Draw a guideline around the top and bottom edge using the ruler or a compass. Cut a piece of binding to fit the top edge of the shade and square off one end of the binding. Starting at the squared end, apply glue to the lower half of the first few inches. Press the binding into place, starting $\frac{1}{4}$ inch to the left of the back seam and just covering the marked line. Allow the glue to set for a minute. Continue to apply the glue to the lower half of the binding, working in 9- to 10-inch segments, holding the binding away from the shade. Press the binding in place as before, making sure it is smooth and even. Continue until you reach the back seam. Using the back seam as a guide, trim the binding perpendicular to the edge of the shade. Apply glue to the full width of the binding at the back seam. Overlap the edges and press into place. [photo H]

12 ON THE TOP RING ONLY, USE THE SCISSORS TO MAKE SMALL slashes in the binding where the spokes connect to the wire ring. Apply a thin, even coat of glue to the inside half of the binding and press in place to the inside of the shade, rolling and molding the binding over the top of the wire. Turning the shade on its side, reach inside the shade and use your fingernail to crease the edge of the binding around the wire. Repeat for the bottom edge, omitting the slashes for the spokes.

picking shade materials

Many heavy papers and fabrics make unique lamp shades. To preview how it will look, hold the paper or fabric up to a lightbulb. You will be able to see immediately if the paper or fabric works well under the light. Look for fabric that is evenly woven with no slubs or knots (unless it is a slubbed silk, which is meant to be that way). Printed fabric or paper should be consistently colored, not blotchy. With textured papers eliminate any that have uneven thick and thin areas that will show up when the light is on. Make sure to ask a salesperson whether your choice of paper is heat resistant.

bindings for shades

Other popular bindings for lamp shades are ⅝-inch grosgrain ribbon or cotton twill tape. Polyester ribbons should be avoided, as they repel glue. Different kinds of decorative braids can also be used, though on a busy shade a simple trim is more effective. On a solid-color fabric shade a binding made with the same fabric would be preferable.

Pressed Glass Lamps

LAMPS EXACTLY LIKE THESE ARE FREQUENT FINDS AT FLEA MARKETS, HOUSE SALES, AND THRIFT SHOPS. IN FACT, MORE THAN ONCE, I'VE BOUGHT A SINGLE LAMP AND THEN A FEW WEEKS LATER COME ACROSS A MATCHING ONE AT A SALE OR FLEA MARKET. MY FAVORITES ARE THOSE OF CLEAR GLASS. THEY'RE SO PRETTY AND USEFUL THAT I'VE DECIDED TO SNAP UP EACH ONE THAT I SEE. YOU CAN EVEN DISASSEMBLE THEM AND RECOMBINE THE PARTS TO MAKE NEW LAMPS. TO REFURBISH LAMPS LIKE THESE IS A SIMPLE MATTER. USE THE TECHNIQUES BELOW TO RESTORE THE LUSTER TO ANY METAL PARTS THAT HAVE BECOME RUSTY AND PITTED. EACH PIECE SHOULD BE NUMBERED BEFORE YOU TAKE THE LAMP TOTALLY APART SO IT CAN BE EASILY REASSEMBLED LATER.

materials

Lamps	Chrome or glossy finish spray paint
Masking tape	Ammonia
Permanent marker	Old toothbrush
Wire cutters	Scrub pad
Screwdriver	White vinegar
Steel wool	Cord with attached plug
Dish soap	

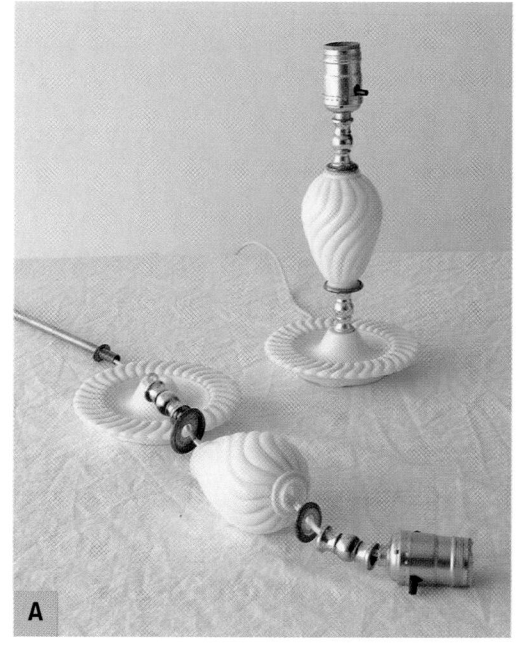
A

1 TAKE THE LAMP APART BY UNSCREWING THE LOCK NUT holding the threaded rod in place under the base of the lamp. When you unscrew the socket as well, the lamp will start to separate into sections. Stick a piece of masking tape onto each piece and number sequentially with the marker. If you have a pair of lamps, take them apart one at a time, leaving one intact for reference. [photo A]

2 IF THE CORD NEEDS REPLACING, CUT AT THE BOTTOM OF THE lamp. Squeeze the socket shell on the side where the word ***press*** is imprinted, and lift it off the socket base cap. Remove the insulating sleeve and loosen the terminal screws to disconnect the old wires. Pull the old cord through the lamp. Save the original socket. If it's in good condition, it can be reused. [photo B]

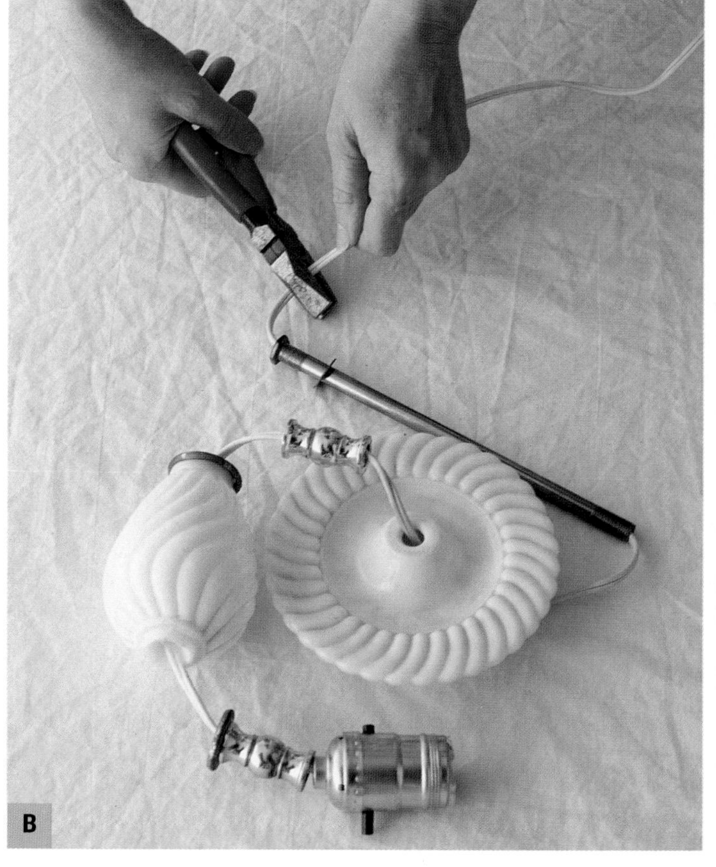
B

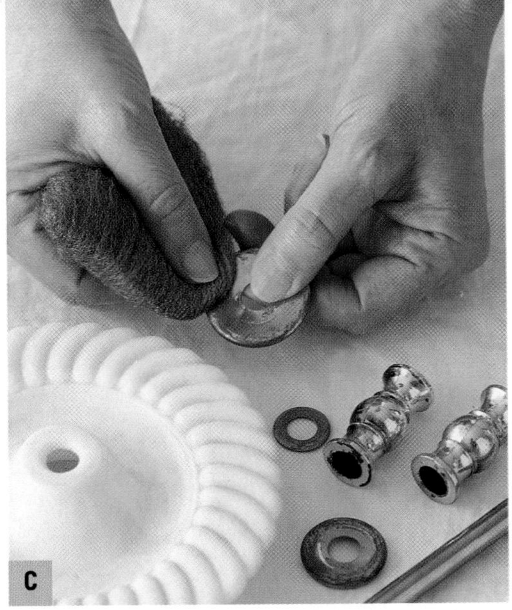
C

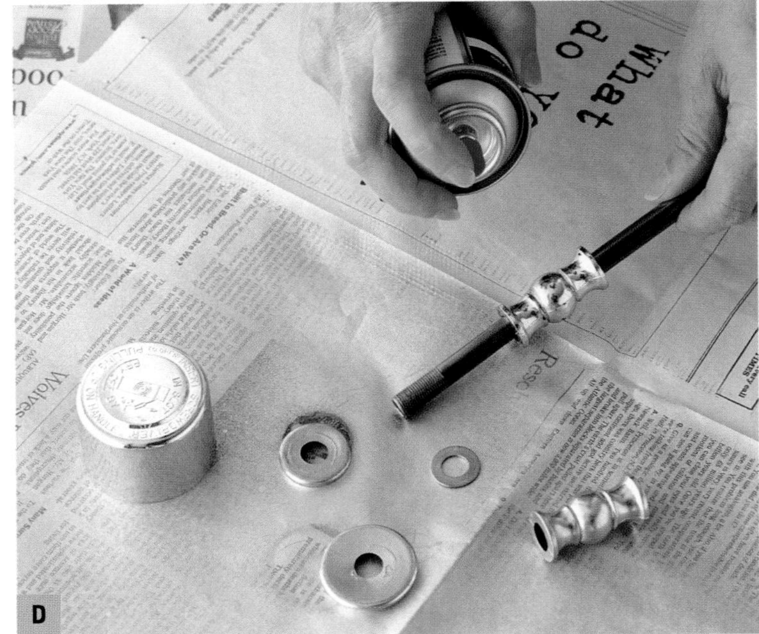
D

3 CLEAN ANY RUST OFF THE METAL PARTS WITH STEEL WOOL. Wash any nonmetal parts as well as the metal parts in dish soap and water. Rinse well and let everything dry. [photo C]

4 SPRAY THE NONGLASS AND METAL PIECES WITH 2 OR 3 coats of the chrome (or glossy) spray paint following the directions on the can, letting them dry between coats. When spray painting the pieces, stick the numbered piece of masking tape in front of each piece on the paper before you spray paint it. Let dry completely. [photo D]

E

5 CLEAN ALL THE GLASS PIECES THOROUGHLY INSIDE AND OUT using water with dish soap and a little ammonia added. Use the old toothbrush to scrub the dirt out of crevices. A design painted on milk glass can be removed by scrubbing with a synthetic scrubbing pad and hot soapy water. When everything is clean fill the sink with cool water. Add a small amount of white vinegar to the water and rinse the pieces carefully. Dry everything thoroughly. Reassemble the lamp and rewire the lamp and socket following the directions on pages 26–27. [photos E and F]

F

6 ADD A PURCHASED SHADE, OR MAKE YOUR OWN USING THE instructions on pages 40–43. [photo F]

Fabric Lamp Shade

SIMPLE MILK GLASS BASES LIKE THESE CAN BE PAIRED WITH ALMOST ANY FABRIC THAT SUITS YOUR COLOR AND DECORATING SCHEME. FOR A FRESH LOOK IN A LITTLE GIRL'S BEDROOM CHOOSE A SMALL SCALE FLORAL ON A LIGHT BACKGROUND. USE A COTTAGEY, FLOWER PRINT TO ADD A COZY TOUCH TO AN ADULT'S BEDROOM. A ½-INCH GINGHAM CHECK MAKES FOR AN INFORMAL, COUNTRY-INSPIRED SHADE. TICKING (USED ON THE SHADES HERE) IS ONE OF MY ALL-TIME FAVORITE FABRICS. IT HAS ITS OWN SPECIAL APPEAL—DEPENDING ON ITS SETTING IT CAN ADD AN UNDERSTATED CHARM TO A MORE FORMAL INTERIOR OR A TOUCH OF REFINEMENT TO A MORE CASUAL SCHEME. WHEN USING PATTERNED FABRIC MAKE SURE TO BIND THE EDGES WITH A CONTRASTING COLOR FOR A MORE FINISHED LOOK.

materials

Existing lamp shade (or 1 set of top and bottom lamp shade rings and a predrafted arc pattern to fit rings)
Metal straightedge
Permanent marker
Brown kraft paper
Scissors
Craft knife
Heat-resistant pressure-sensitive styrene
Small weights
Soft lead pencil
1 yard fabric for lamp shade
Soft white eraser
Craft glue
Square-tipped artist's brush
Clothespins
Wax paper
Clear plastic ruler or compass
Cotton twill tape, $^{13}/_{16}$ inch wide

1 TO MAKE YOUR OWN ARC PATTERN BASED ON AN EXISTING shade, with the straightedge and the marker, draw a line slightly longer than the height of the shade at the lower left corner of a piece of brown kraft paper. Align the seam of the lamp shade with that line. Roll the lamp shade to the right, tracing its path at the top and bottom edges along the paper, marking the outline of the shade as you continue to roll it over the surface. When you reach the seam again, stop and make a vertical mark on the paper at the top and bottom to indicate the back seam line. Remove the shade from the paper. Connect the vertical marks and add ½ inch to the right edge of the pattern for the back seam overlap. The resulting arc pattern can be cut out, using scissors for the curves and a straightedge and craft knife for the straight ends. [photo A]

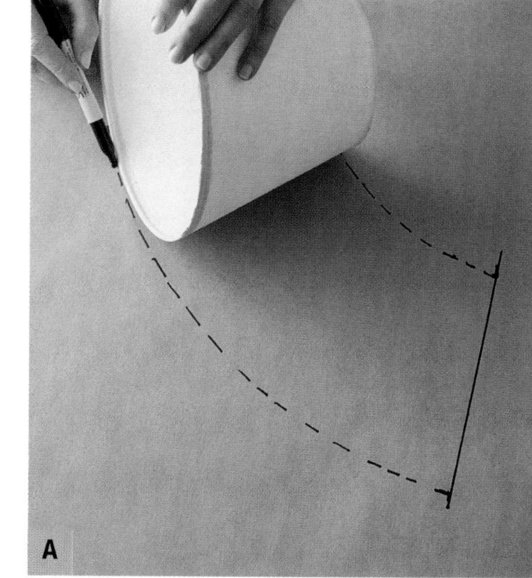
A

2 LAY THE PATTERN ON THE STYRENE SIDE OF THE laminating material. Place weights on the pattern to keep it from moving and trace around the outside edges with the pencil. Mark the ½-inch seam allowance as well. Cut out the arc with the scissors and craft knife as above. Erase any pencil lines except for the seam allowance.

3 IRON THE FABRIC IF NEEDED AND PLACE IT FACE-down on the work surface. Peel a few inches of the protective paper backing from the right-hand edge of the styrene backing and position it on the fabric, paper-side down, to line up with the straight edge (selvage) of the fabric. Reach under the arc and remove the remaining protective covering while smoothing the arc into place on the fabric. [photo B]

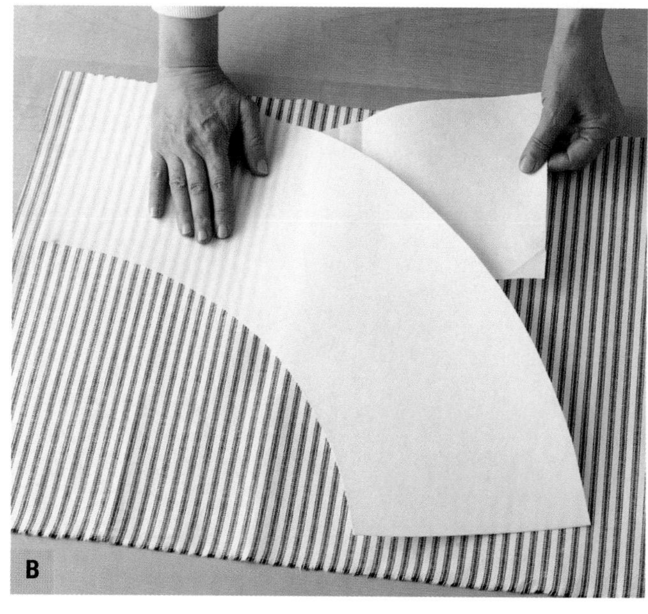
B

C

4 CUT THE EXCESS FABRIC AWAY FROM THE laminated arc, allowing ½-inch strip of extra fabric at the right-hand edge for folding to the inside. With the brush, apply a thin, even coat of glue along the entire length of the ½-inch strip and fold the fabric to the inside of the shade. Press in place and let dry for a few minutes. [photo C]

5 IF YOU ARE USING THE RINGS FROM THE original shade, remove the material and sand off any remaining adhesive. Place the rings on a flat surface. If they are not flat, bend gently to straighten.

6 HOLD THE BOTTOM SPOKELESS WIRE RING in one hand. Place the bottom center front of the arc on the wire ring and fasten the edge to the ring with a clothespin. Fit the shade into shape around the ring, fastening it as you go with the clothespins, working toward the left until you reach the outside edge. Return to the center front and fit the right half of the shade to the ring. Repeat for the top ring. Adjust the fit so the top and bottom of the shade fit evenly around the edge of the rings and there are no gaps. With the back seam facing you, lightly mark with pencil the top and bottom seam overlap. [see page 31, photo E]

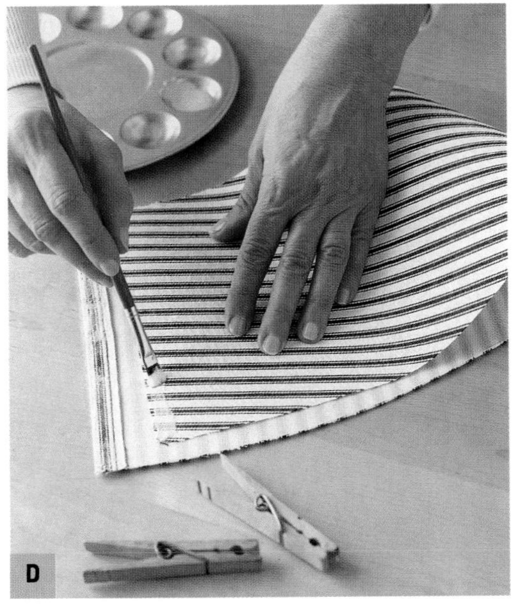
D

7 REMOVE THE CLOTHESPINS AND SET THE RINGS ASIDE. Place the shade on a work surface with the right side up. Check that the seam allowance is straight. Turn the shade over and with the wrong side faceup apply a thin, even coat of glue along the entire length of the back seam overlap, keeping within the line of the inside edge of the seam allowance. Lifting the edge of the shade, hold it so the right side is facing you and apply a thin, even coat of glue along the entire length of the seam allowance on the outside (right side). [photo D]

8 BENDING THE SHADE INTO SHAPE, LINE UP THE TOP EDGE along the pencil mark and fasten with a clothespin. Secure the bottom edge in the same fashion. Hold the glued seam together for a few minutes until the glue sets, then place, seam-side down, on a piece of wax paper. Remove the clothespins and place small weights along the back seam. Let dry for 15 to 20 minutes, removing the weights when the glue is completely dry.

9 STAND THE SHADE ON THE WORK SURFACE WITH the top resting on the table. Apply a thin line of glue along the bottom inside edge of the shade, rotating the shade as you work. Ease the bottom ring into place starting at the center front, positioning the weld in the ring slightly to the right of the back seam. Fasten the ring in place with the clothespins, making sure the ring is positioned evenly inside the shade. Repeat with the top ring, pulling the ring up from inside the shade and positioning one of the top ring's 3 spokes in line with the back seam of the shade. Let the glue dry for 20 minutes and then remove the clothespins. [see page 32, photo G]

10 BIND THE TOP AND BOTTOM EDGES OF THE SHADE to the wire rings with cotton twill tape. Draw a guideline around the top and bottom edge, using a clear plastic ruler or a compass. Cut a piece of tape to fit the top edge of the shade; square off one end of the tape. Starting at the squared end, apply glue to the lower half of the first few inches. Press the tape into place, starting ¼ inch to the left of the back seam and just covering the marked line. Allow the glue to set for 1 minute. Continue to apply the glue to the lower half of the tape, working in 9- to 10-inch segments, holding the tape away from the shade. Press the tape in place as before, making sure it is smooth and even. Continue until you reach the back seam. Using the back seam as a guide, trim the tape perpendicular to the edge of the shade. Apply glue to the full width of the tape at the back seam. Overlap the edges and press into place. [see page 32, photo H]

11 ON THE TOP RING ONLY, USE THE SCISSORS TO MAKE SMALL slashes in the tape where the spokes connect to the wire ring. Apply a thin, even coat of glue to the inside half of the tape and press in place to the inside of the shade, rolling and molding the tape over the top of the wire. Turning the shade on its side, reach inside the shade and use your fingernail to crease the edge of the tape around the wire. Repeat for the bottom edge, omitting the slashes for the spokes.

E

applying a decorative trim

Additional decorative trims, such as ⅜-inch velvet ribbon or bias-fold trim, can be used to further embellish the lamp shade. Leave a 1-inch tail at the starting end of the trim. Apply glue to the underside of the first few inches. Press in place on the top edge of the shade, starting the glued portion ½ inch to the right of the back seam. The bottom edge of the decorative trim should just cover the binding. Continue around the shade, following gluing directions as for the tape above, until you are within 1½ inches of the back seam. Allow the unglued end of the decorative trim to lay over the starting tail. Using a small sharp scissors, cut through both layers of trim perpendicular to the edge of the shade. Glue the ends and press into place. Repeat on the bottom. [photo E]

YOU CAN USE EITHER A PREDRAFTED ARC PATTERN FROM A LAMP SUPPLY SOURCE OR MAKE YOUR OWN ARC PATTERN AS EXPLAINED BELOW.

Here is an easy formula for making an arc pattern for a basic cone-shaped lamp shade. Start by measuring the diameters of the top and bottom rings. You'll also need to determine the height of the proposed lamp shade. With these measurements and a simple yardstick compass, you'll be able to create an arc pattern that can be used to make a custom-sized shade to fit your lamp. If you want to save the pattern, it can be drafted on a large piece of paper, cut out, and then traced onto your material (see page 40), or you can draft the pattern directly onto the styrene backing or any other lamp-shade material of your choice.

1 Draw a vertical line corresponding to the height of the lampshade (AB in the diagram).

2 Draw two lines corresponding to the diameters of the bottom ring (CD) and the top ring (EF), perpendicular to and centered on the top and bottom ends of the vertical (AB) line.

3 Draw a line connecting points D and F, extending it up about two times its length. Repeat for the other side, connecting points C and E.

4 Label as X the point where DF crosses CE.

5 Calculate the length of the bottom arc (DH) by multiplying the length of the line CD by pi (3.14) and adding ½ inch for the side seam overlap. Use the yardstick compass to draw the bottom arc (DH). Anchor the compass point on X and place the pencil on D, moving the pencil to the left to scribe a semicircle (or arc) of that length. Check the length measurement with a tape measure. This forms the bottom arc (DH) for the shade pattern.

6 Repeat for the top arc by multiplying the length of the line EF by pi (3.14) and adding ½ inch for overlap. Use this measurement for the length of the top arc (FI), which can be drawn by placing the compass point on X and the pencil on F. Use a tape measure to check the length.

7 Cut out the pattern (or actual shade) using a metal ruler and craft knife for the straight edges and scissors for the curves.

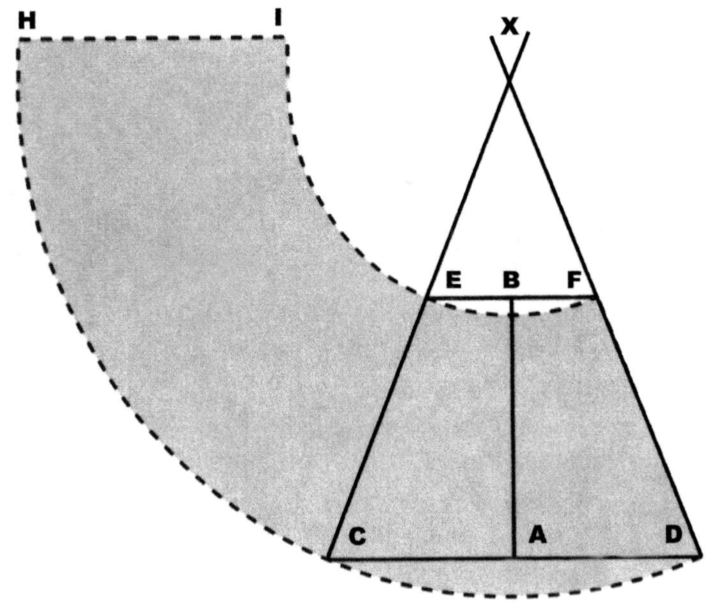

Glass and Metal Chandelier

I ACQUIRED THIS 1950S CHANDELIER ON A FAMILY TRIP TO THE MIDWEST THREE YEARS AGO, WHEN SOME FRIENDS WHO HAD MOVED INTO A NEW HOUSE WHERE IT HAD ORIGINALLY HUNG OFFERED IT TO ME. OF COURSE I HAD TO TAKE IT. THE CHANDELIER WASN'T IN TERRIBLE SHAPE, JUST A LITTLE DARK AND DINGY. IN A DIFFERENT HOME THAN OURS IT MIGHT HAVE LOOKED FINE, BUT I WANTED SOMETHING LIGHTER AND PRETTIER. I DECIDED TO TRY PAINTING IT BLUE AND GREEN AND IVORY IN AN ATTEMPT TO RECREATE THE COLORFUL VENETIAN GLASS CHANDELIERS I FELL IN LOVE WITH ON A TRIP TO ITALY YEARS AGO.

ANYTHING MADE OF METAL, NOT JUST CHANDELIERS, CAN BE PAINTED IN A SIMILAR FASHION. LOOK FOR SMALL GARDEN TABLES, HANGING SHELVES, AND HOLDERS FOR PLANTS DECORATED WITH NATURAL FORMS LIKE LEAVES OR FLOWERS.

materials

Chandelier
Screwdriver
Dish soap
Ammonia
Old toothbrush
Fine-grade steel wool
Masking tape
Ivory spray paint
Small artist's brush
Sign painter's lettering paint in bright green and robin's egg blue
¼ yard off-white linen fabric
Sewing machine or hand sewing needle
Cotton thread

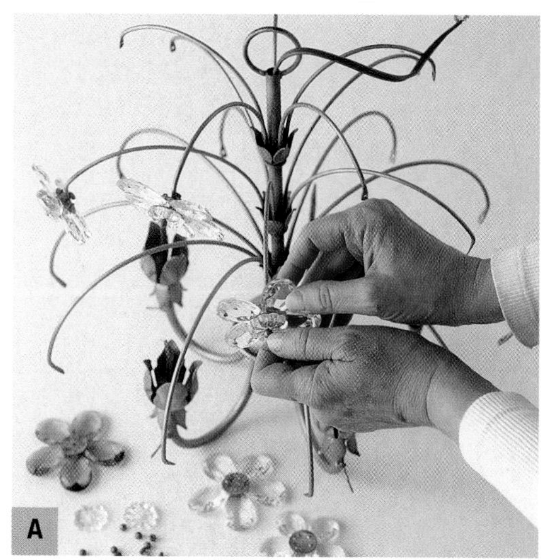
A

1 REMOVE THE DECORATIVE PLASTIC SLEEVES AND THE inside insulating sleeves from the candle sockets at the base of each arm. Loosen the terminal screws on either side of the socket and detach the wires from the screws. Unscrew the candle sockets from the threaded rods in each arm. Lift off and set aside. Carefully inspect the wiring; if it is obviously worn or damaged, the chandelier will need to be rewired. Take the rest of the chandelier apart by unscrewing the small threaded round head pins holding the decorative glass florets in place. Set aside all of the parts. [photo A]

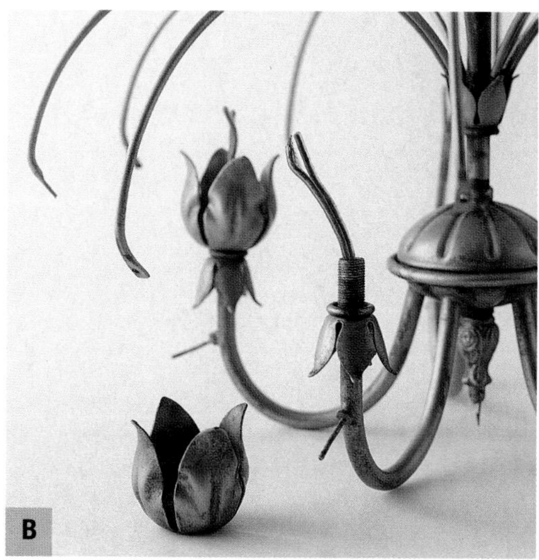
B

2 AFTER REMOVING THE CANDLE SOCKETS, LIFT OFF AND SET aside the 2 leaf-shaped round metal pieces and the metal ring that sit at the base of each arm. [photo B]

3 CLEAN ALL THE GLASS PIECES THOROUGHLY USING WATER with dish soap and a little ammonia. An old toothbrush can be useful for scrubbing the dirt out of crevices. Rinse well and let dry. Clean all the metal parts of the lamp and prepare the metal surface for spray painting by rubbing down all the pieces with fine-grade steel wool.

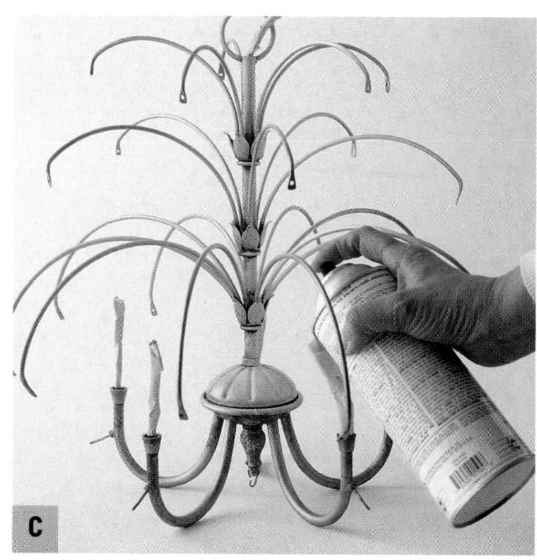
C

4 WRAP ALL THE EXPOSED WIRING WITH MASKING TAPE TO protect it from the spray paint. Spray the metal armature of the chandelier with 2 or 3 coats of ivory spray paint, letting the paint dry between each coat. Make sure to spray the underneath areas as well. Let dry completely. [photo C]

5 WITH THE SMALL ARTIST'S BRUSH, PAINT THE LARGER METAL leaf-shaped pieces with 2 coats (letting dry between coats) of the bright green paint and the smaller metal leaf-shaped pieces and the metal rings with 2 coats of the robin's egg blue paint. [photo D]

D

6 USE THE SMALL ARTIST'S BRUSH TO PAINT the small details on the chandelier armature with 2 coats of paint and the dome-shaped centerpiece with 2 coats. Let everything dry completely. [photo E]

7 TO REASSEMBLE THE LAMP, FIRST PUT THE painted leaf-shaped pieces and rings back on the arms, then replace the candle sockets. Reattach the lamp wires to the candle sockets following the directions on page 23. Lastly, reattach the glass florets to the metal brackets.

8 CUT A LONG RECTANGLE OUT OF THE LINEN fabric, about 5 inches wide and 8 inches longer than the hanging chain. Sew a narrow hem at the top and bottom and fold in half the long way with the right sides together. Sew the edges together to make a tube that will fit over the chain. Turn right-side-out and slip over the chain before hanging the lamp.

E

chairs

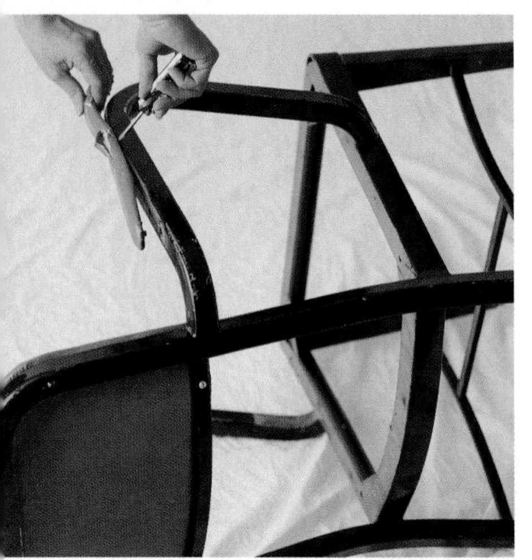

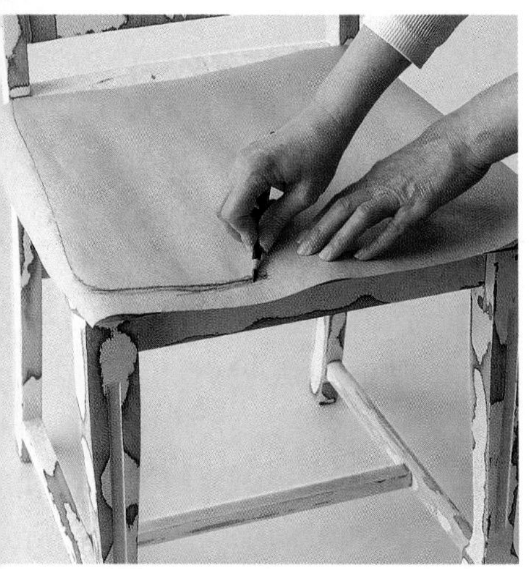

i've always found it easy to

ferret out worn but charming chairs and benches at thrift stores, especially the bigger ones that offer an extensive selection of furniture. Among my favorite finds were a dark green velvet boudoir chair with a down-stuffed seat cushion, a classic fifties lounge chair in chartreuse green Naugahyde, a couple of quirky benches, and numerous wooden dining room and kitchen chairs. The velvet chair was slightly worn but still far from shabby and it had an air of fading glamour, as if it had once dwelt in the bedroom of an old romantic Hollywood movie. The fifties chair is exactly like those I've seen since selling for much more in tony retro furniture stores.

Even better bargains were the chairs I've found free for the taking in Dumpsters or trash piles. People frequently discard old wooden kitchen-type chairs when all they really need are some simple repairs. I've often rescued slightly broken chairs from the trash in order to reconstruct them. Basic repairs are very easy to accomplish; usually the joints on the legs or sides will need to be reglued. If you take the time to thoroughly clean the joints before regluing and allow the glue to dry thoroughly, you can easily return the chair to working order, making it ready to strip or paint as you choose.

Wooden chairs are the easiest to make over—all it really takes to transform them is a few coats of paint. They have the advantage of

being easy to repaint if you decide to change your color scheme. Cane seats can be painted over as well. For an antique look, the finish can be slightly distressed. Adding matching upholstered seats or cushions, in addition to the paint, can tie different shapes together. This way a variety of chairs can bring a creative edge to a dining room or kitchen table without looking too disorganized. I personally find using different shapes of chairs much more fun than a traditional matching set.

As for upholstered pieces, you should keep your eye out for two kinds of finds: fine, well-made pieces and not-so-well-made but pleasing and useful pieces. A good quality, well-made piece of upholstered furniture is always worth buying, even if you can't stand the fabric. The cost of restoring and/or recovering is generally far less than the cost of a comparable new piece. Sometimes you'll come across a pleasant and useful piece but one that's not particularly well made—the workmanship is so-so, the materials of inferior quality. Even so, it can be worth buying and refurbishing on the cheap—until you can replace it with something better. I have one upholstered club chair that I bought for $35; it had a nice shape and was very comfortable but was covered in the most awful cheap fabric and was definitely not a good piece of furniture. But I had a slipcover made for it and it looks just fine—as a matter of fact, I've always regretted not buying the matching one.

Metal Office Chair

OLD METAL OFFICE FURNITURE, ESPECIALLY PIECES THAT HAVE BEEN STRIPPED DOWN TO THE BASE METAL, HAVE BECOME MUCH IN DEMAND. BUT YOU CAN STILL FIND UNREFINISHED PIECES LIKE THIS DESK CHAIR AT BARGAIN PRICES. IT WASN'T DIFFICULT TO REMOVE THE PAINT THAT HAD BEEN APPLIED OVER THE METAL FRAME, BUT THE PROCESS OF STRIPPING THE FRAME DOWN TO THE BARE METAL AFTERWARD WAS RATHER TIME CONSUMING. THE RESULTS ARE MORE THAN WORTH IT, AS THE UNCOVERED METAL LENDS A GREAT DEAL OF CHIC TO THE PIECE. THE TRADITIONAL, ROMANTIC TOILE FABRIC CONTRASTS STYLISHLY WITH THE SLEEK METAL, AN UNEXPECTED COMBINATION OF TWO DISPARATE ELEMENTS THAT WORKS. A SOLID-COLOR FABRIC, LIKE ULTRASUEDE, A STURDY TEXTURED COTTON, OR REAL LEATHER, WOULD LOOK JUST AS GOOD. YOU CAN RE-COVER THE CHAIR YOURSELF BUT I WOULD SUGGEST SENDING THE PIECE OUT TO BE REUPHOLSTERED AS RE-COVERING METAL FURNITURE REQUIRES SLIGHTLY DIFFERENT METHODS THAN THOSE USED ON A MORE TRADITIONAL PIECE BECAUSE THE UNDER PART IS METAL. IN THIS CASE, THE COST OF HAVING THE CHAIR PROFESSIONALLY RE-COVERED SEEMED VERY REASONABLE AS THE CHAIR INITIALLY COST ONLY $5 AT THE SALVATION ARMY.

materials

Metal desk chair	Power drill with medium wire brush wheel
Screwdriver	Spray lacquer
Paint remover	Black and white toile fabric
Household paintbrush	¼-inch plywood (optional)
Putty knife	
Steel wool	

1 TAKE THE UPHOLSTERED SEAT AND ARMRESTS OFF THE chair by removing the screws that are holding them in place from the underside of the metal frame. The backrest is held in place with screws also, but it has metal tabs on the backside as well that slide into slots on the top edge of the frame. Remove the screws first, then the backrest can drop down and out of the frame. Set the upholstered pieces aside. [photo A]

2 REMOVE THE PAINT FROM THE FRAME WITH A NONTOXIC paint remover, following the directions on the container. Scrape off old paint with the putty knife. Make sure to work outside or in a

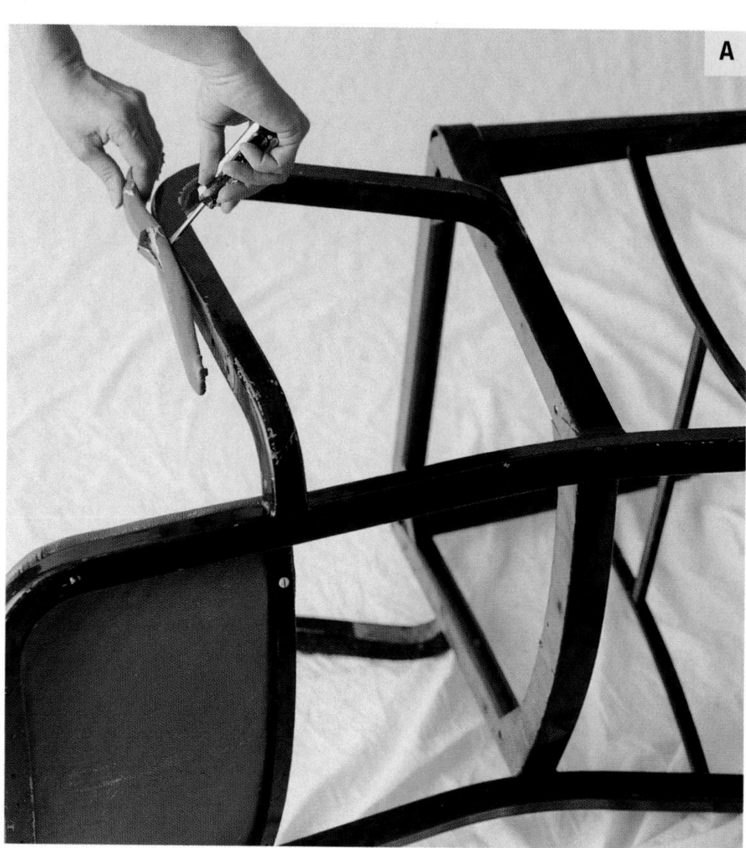
A

stripping and polishing metal furniture

Working on one small section (like a leg) at a time, apply paint remover. Work outside or in a well-ventilated space and wear a protective mask. After 15 minutes the paint will start to soften and appear crinkled. Scrape off as much of the softened paint as you can with a putty knife, then use a medium-grade steel wool pad to remove the rest. Discard the pad when it fills up with paint. If necessary, apply a second coat of paint remover and repeat the process. Attach a medium steel wire brush to a power drill and work slowly and evenly over the surface of the frame. Finish smoothing and polishing the surface, working evenly back and forth across the frame to achieve an overall brushed, satin finish. Be sure to keep the drill moving over the frame to ensure a uniform-looking brushed pattern. Wipe down with a clean cloth and spray with clear satin lacquer if desired.

well-ventilated space and wear a protective mask, if needed. Any stubborn areas can be gone over with steel wool. Polish the frame using the power drill with a wire brush attachment to give the metal a brushed finish. When you have achieved the desired finish, spray the frame with lacquer to protect it. (See sidebar.) [photo B]

3 MAKE NEW COVERS FOR THE SEAT, BACKREST, AND armrests by taking them apart to use as patterns for the new covers. The original padding can usually be reused. One tip that will help: Cut a new bottom for the drop-in chair seat out of $\frac{1}{4}$-inch-thick plywood to replace the existing metal seat bottom. Alternatively, bring the upholstered pieces—and the frame—to an upholsterer to have the pieces re-covered and the chair reassembled. If you do want to give it a try yourself, consult a good reference book on upholstery techniques (see Resources, pages 155–56). [photo C]

B

C

Wooden Kitchen Chair

I SPOTTED THIS CHAIR ON THE CURB ONE NIGHT AND OF COURSE STOPPED TO PICK IT UP. THE SOLE SURVIVOR OF A VINTAGE FORTIES KITCHEN SET, THE CHAIR'S ATTRACTIVE ARCHITECTURALLY SHAPED BACK WAS STILL APPARENT BENEATH THE MANY LAYERS OF PAINT ACQUIRED OVER THE YEARS. BECAUSE CHAIRS FROM THIS PERIOD ARE SO STURDY, MY DUMPSTER FIND WAS BASICALLY IN EXCELLENT SHAPE. FOR THE CUSHION, I CHOSE SCRAPS OF VINTAGE FLORAL; THE SOFT CREAMINESS OF THE PAINT PICKS UP THE CREAMY TONES IN THE FLOWERS AND LEAVES IN A VERY PLEASING WAY.

materials

Wooden chair	Printed cotton fabric
Power sander (optional)	Solid-color twill fabric
Sandpaper	Pins
Paint remover	Sewing machine
Acrylic primer	Cotton sewing thread
Household paintbrush	½-inch cotton cording
Satin finish oil-based paint	Iron
Brown paper	½-inch-thick foam cushion insert
Soft lead pencil	Hand sewing needle
Ruler	
Scissors	

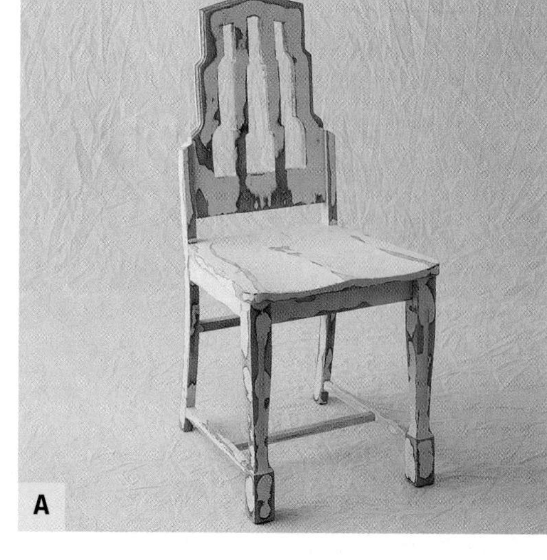

A

1 IF THE EXISTING LAYERS OF PAINT ARE ESPECIALLY THICK, sand the chair with the power sander (make sure to wear a mask) to remove some of the paint and create an even, smooth, nonglossy surface. Alternatively, remove the paint with a nontoxic paint remover. If you choose to remove the paint entirely, prime with an acrylic primer and when dry, sand the surface lightly with fine-grade sandpaper. Paint with 2 coats of the oil-based satin finish paint. Let dry completely. [photo A]

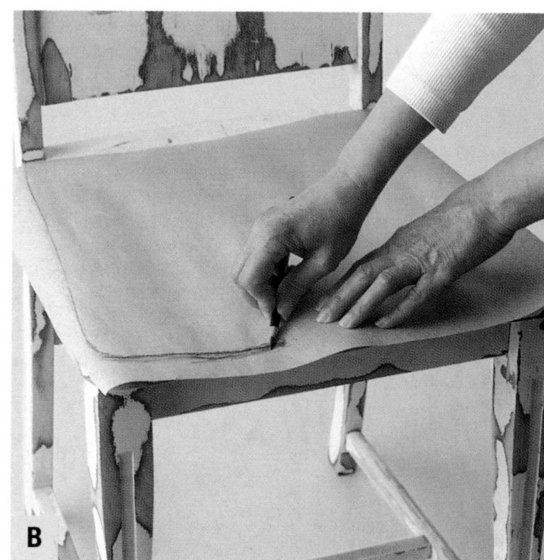

B

2 TO MAKE A PATTERN FOR THE CHAIR CUSHION, PLACE A piece of brown paper on the seat and outline the edges with a soft lead pencil. [photo B]

3 REMOVE THE PAPER PATTERN AND WITH THE RULER AND pencil draw a vertical line down its center. Fold the pattern in half along that line, with the traced outline facing out. Working on one half, straighten out the lines. Leave the paper folded in half and cut around the new line with scissors. Unfold the pattern and lay on the chair seat to check, making any adjustments. [photo C]

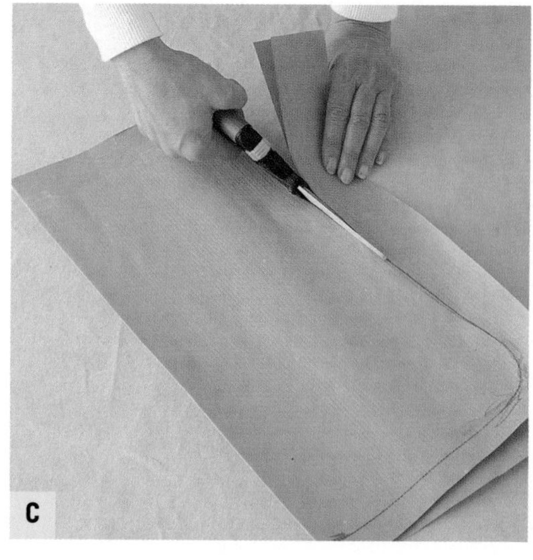

C

4 PLACE THE PATTERN ON THE PRINTED FABRIC AND CAREFULLY center the motif; secure with pins. Cut out the top cushion cover. Cut out the bottom cushion cover from the solid-color fabric. Make up the piping as follows: Find the cross grain or bias by folding a corner of the solid fabric up to the opposite selvage in a triangle. The fold will form a 45-degree angle to the selvage. The line formed by the fold is the bias or cross grain of the fabric. With a pencil, mark parallel lines starting at the fold at 1½-inch intervals on the solid fabric. Cut enough 1½-inch-wide-bias strips to fit around the chair cushion and to make 4 chair ties.

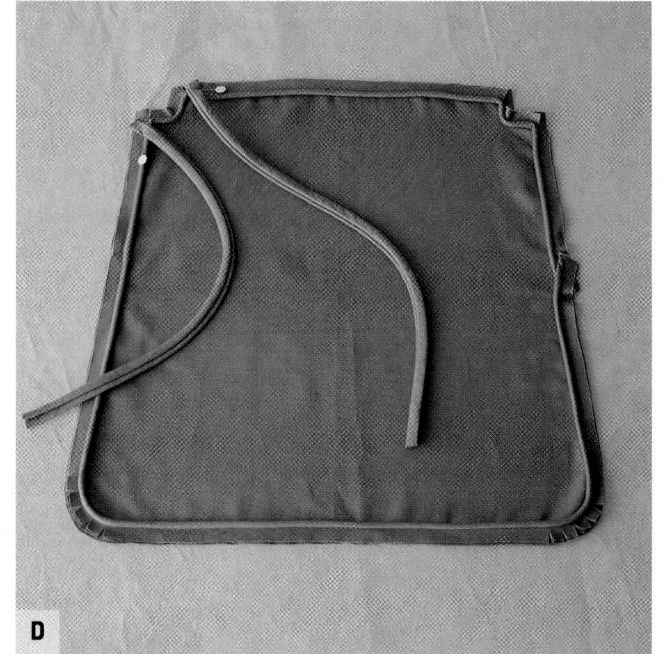

D

E

fabric notebook

5 TO JOIN THE BIAS STRIPS TOGETHER, CUT THE ENDS AT A right angle and overlap the 2 ends, right sides together at right (90-degree) angles to each other. Machine stitch across the diagonal, trim off the corner, and press open. Repeat with the other strips until you have enough to fit around the cushion. To make the piping, lay the cord in the center of the wrong side of the bias strip and fold in half. Using a zipper foot, machine stitch as close to the cord as possible. Make the cushion ties out of four 18-inch-long strips of bias. Turn the raw edges to the inside and top stitch on the right side.

6 WITH THE RAW EDGES TOGETHER, PIN THE PIPING TO THE right side of the bottom cushion cover and machine stitch, allowing a $\frac{1}{2}$-inch seam allowance. Sew 2 chair ties into the seam allowance at each back corner at the same time. Snip the piping seam allowance around the curves and when turning the corners allow the piping to lay flat. [photo D]

7 Lay the top cushion cover underneath the bottom with the right sides together and machine stitch following the previous stitching line, leaving an opening in the back to insert the pad. Trim the fabric at the corners, turn right side out, and press. Insert the foam cushion into the cushion cover and hand-sew the opening closed using a needle and cotton thread to match. Knot the exposed end of each chair tie and trim the raw edge as close to the knot as possible. [photo E]

Lawn Chairs

I BOUGHT THESE TWO LAWN CHAIRS AT COMPLETELY DIFFERENT TIMES IN COMPLETELY DIFFERENT PLACES, THE FIRST AT A SMALL FLEA MARKET IN THE COUNTRY AND THE OTHER AT A CHURCH RUMMAGE SALE IN NEW YORK CITY. I HAVE AN ECLECTIC COLLECTION OF OUTDOOR FURNITURE, MOST OF IT PAINTED. AT FIRST I THOUGHT I WOULD PAINT THESE TWO CHAIRS TO MATCH BUT DECIDED INSTEAD TO STRIP THEM AND APPLY A PROTECTIVE TUNG OIL FINISH—THIS KIND OF TREATMENT REQUIRES MUCH LESS UPKEEP. I'M SO DELIGHTED WITH THEIR APPEARANCE THAT I'M NOW PLANNING TO STRIP AND REFINISH THE REST OF MY OUTDOOR PIECES TO MATCH.

STRIPED FABRIC IS TRADITIONALLY USED ON INFORMAL LAWN FURNITURE LIKE THIS. THE HEAVY-DUTY COTTON CANVAS FABRIC IS BOTH PRACTICAL AND CHARMING AND ITS TIGHT WEAVE MAKES IT LESS VULNERABLE TO WEATHER. IF YOU WANT TO USE DIFFERENT COLORS OF STRIPES, KEEP THE BACKGROUND COLOR THE SAME; THAT WAY, THE OVERALL IMPRESSION IS ONE OF UNITY.

materials

Folding lawn chair	Scissors
Paint remover	Pins
Putty knife	Sewing machine
Fine-grade steel wool or sandpaper	Cotton sewing thread to match fabric
Satin finish tung oil	Iron
Soft rag or cheesecloth	Staples/staple gun
Striped cotton canvas	Small hammer
Soft lead pencil	Brass upholstery tacks
Ruler	

A

1 CAREFULLY REMOVE THE OLD FABRIC FROM THE CHAIR AND set aside; these will be your pattern pieces. [photo A]

2 REMOVE THE PAINT FROM THE FRAME WITH A NONTOXIC paint remover, following the directions on the container. Use a putty knife to scrape the paint off. Make sure to work outside or in a well-ventilated space and wear a protective mask, if needed. [photo B]

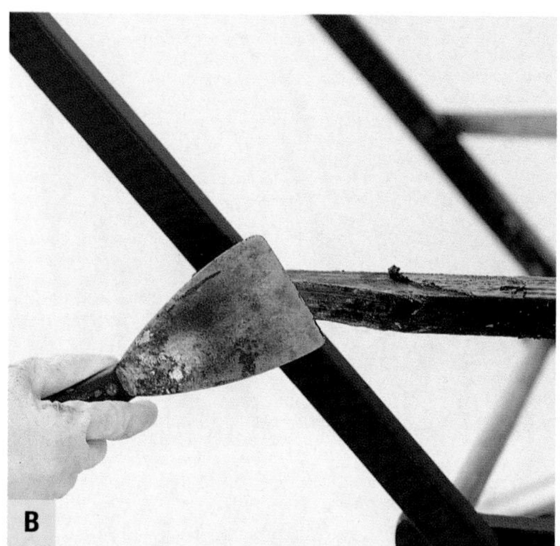
B

3 ANY STUBBORN AREAS OF PAINT CAN BE GONE OVER WITH fine-grade steel wool or sandpaper. When the frame is completely stripped, sand lightly with fine-grade sandpaper. [photo C]

4 APPLY THE TUNG OIL WITH A SOFT RAG following the directions on the container. Repeat as needed, until you have achieved the desired finish. Set the frame aside and let dry completely. [photo D]

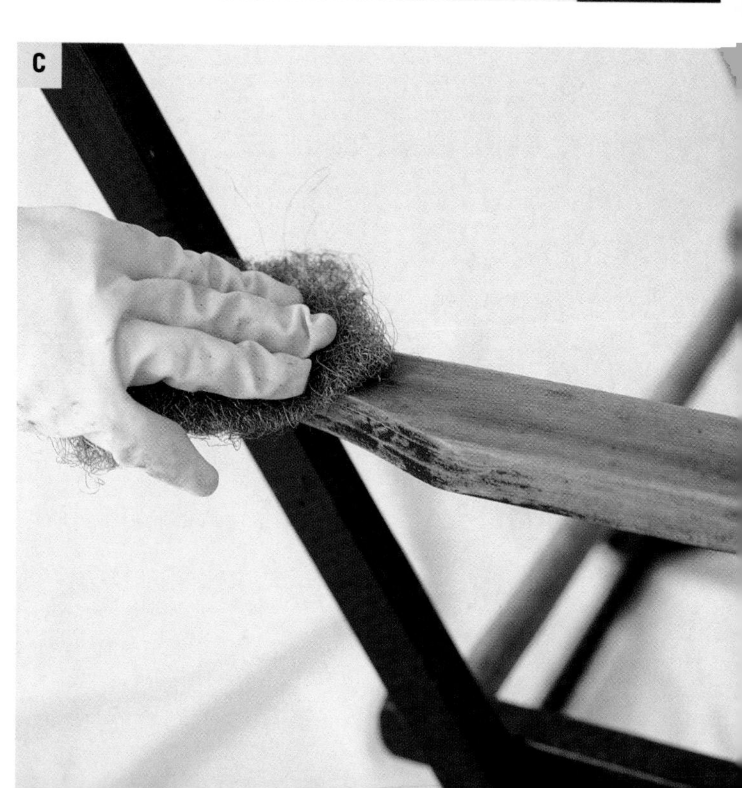
C

5 USE THE ORIGINAL FABRIC PIECES AS patterns for the chair seat and back. Lay the old pieces out on the striped fabric, centering the stripes carefully. Add 2 inches extra to each of the long sides for turning back and hemming. Add 3 inches extra at the top and bottom edges for wrapping and stapling to the frame. If the edge will show, as it does on the backrest section of the blue stripe chair, add an additional inch to each end so the raw edges can be turned under and hidden before tacking. If the originals are missing, just

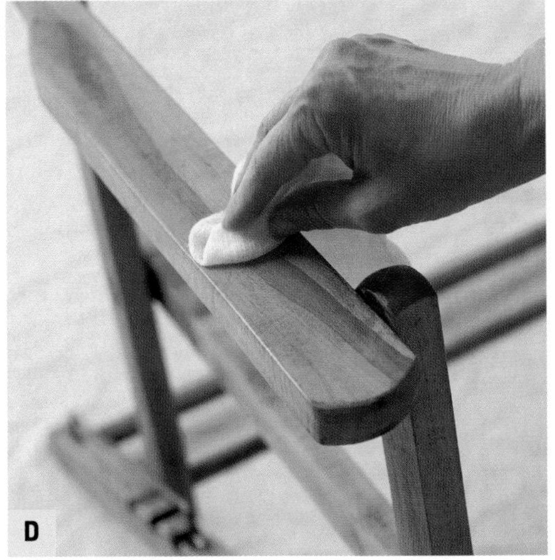

D

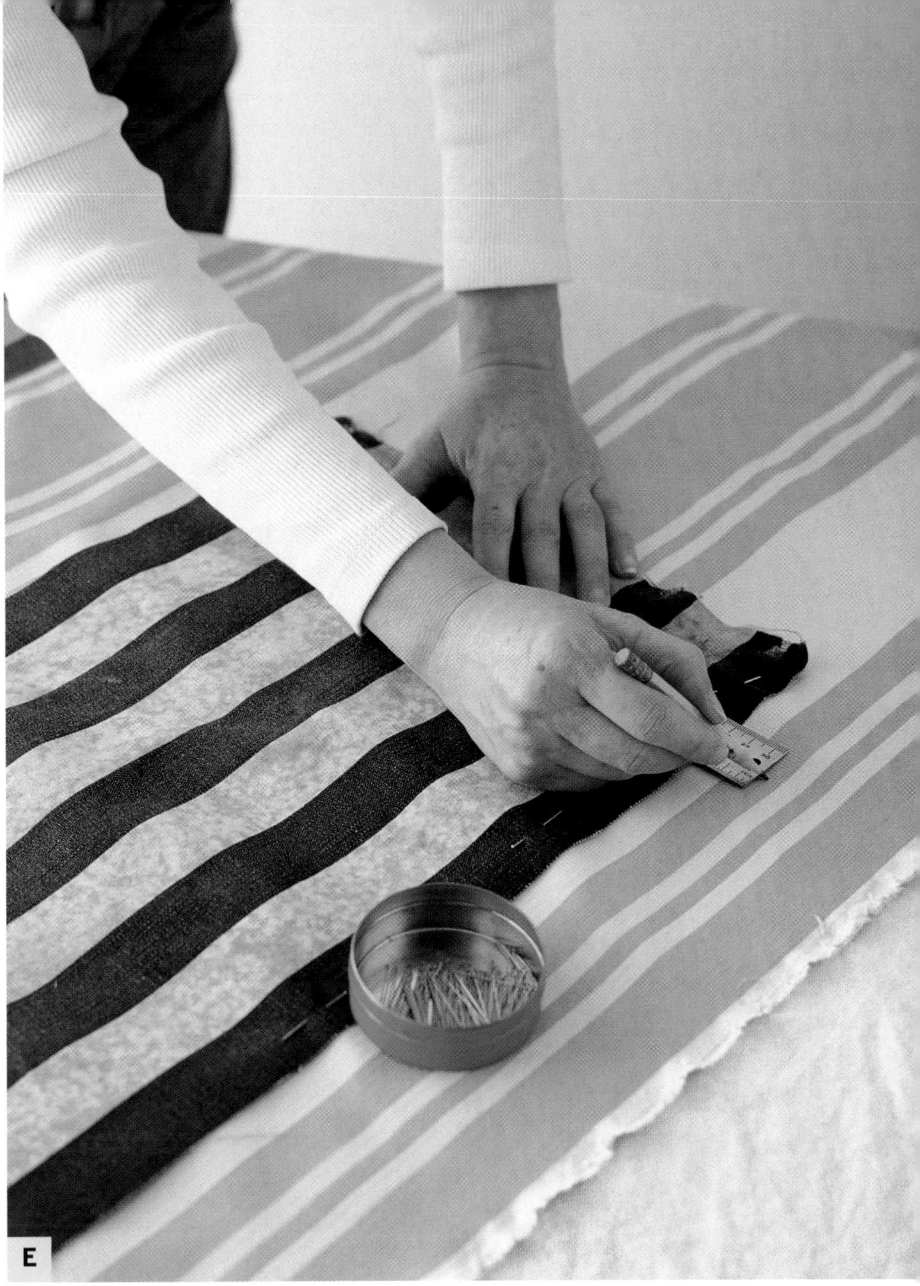

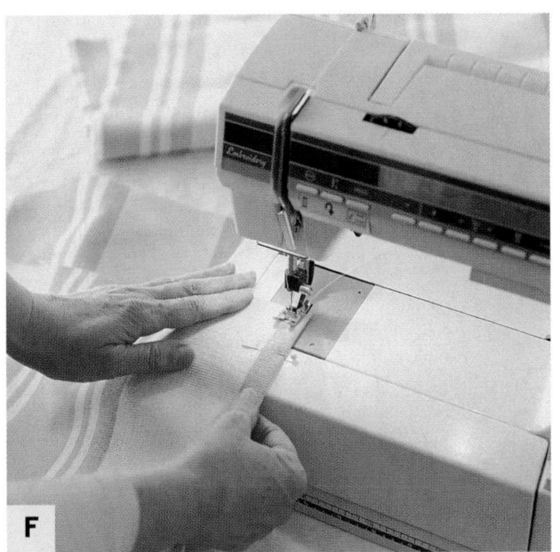

F

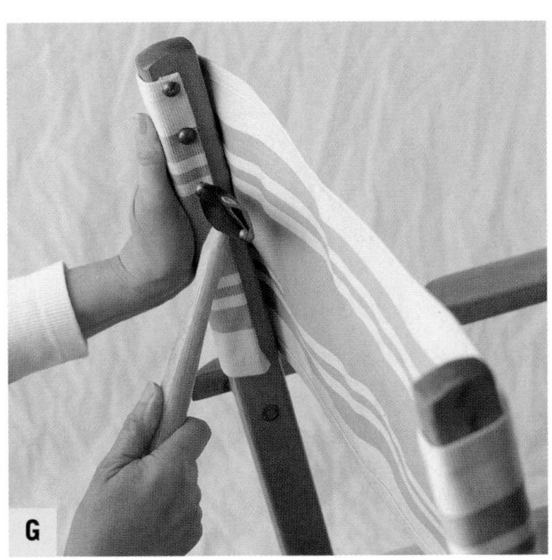

G

E

measure the length and width where the fabric seat or back will go, adding 2 inches to each side for turning under and 3 inches each at the top and bottom for wrapping around and stapling to the frame. [photo E]

6 TURN THE LONG SIDES UNDER 1 INCH AND THEN UNDER the same amount again, pin, and stitch in place by machine. Press the hems carefully with the iron and a damp cloth. [photo F]

7 WRAP THE FABRIC SEATS OVER THE FRAMES AND STAPLE IN place. Wrap the chair back around the posts and turn the raw edges under. Hammer decorative brass upholstery tacks to hold the back in place, setting them about 1 inch apart. [photo G]

Carved Wooden Armchair

SOME OLD FRIENDS ARRIVED AT A BIRTHDAY PARTY I WAS GIVING FOR MY HUSBAND, VINCE, WITH THIS LARGE WOODEN ARMCHAIR IN TOW. THEIR LONGTIME NEIGHBORS HAD BEEN ABOUT TO DISCARD IT AFTER MANY YEARS AS THE PATRIARCH'S "SPECIAL CHAIR." WHILE IT WASN'T REALLY A PRESENT FOR VINCE, MY FRIENDS FELT THIS CHAIR, OWING TO ITS LONG HISTORY, DESERVED A NEW HOME WHERE IT WOULD BE APPRECIATED. WHILE I'M NOT QUITE SURE THAT THE GENTLEMAN WOULD RECOGNIZE HIS BELOVED ARMCHAIR TODAY—PAINTED WHITE AND RECOVERED IN THIS LUSTROUS BLUE STRIPED THAI SILK—I THINK HE WOULD BE GLAD TO SEE THAT IT IS STILL A MUCH LOVED SPOT FOR READING AND CONTEMPLATION. IF YOU WILL BE WORKING WITH A PROFESSIONAL UPHOLSTERER AS I DID, BRING THE CHAIR TO HIM OR HER TO HAVE THE COVERING AND PADDING REMOVED SO THE FRAME CAN BE PAINTED EASILY.

materials

- Wooden armchair
- Pliers
- Screwdriver
- Paint or finish remover (optional)
- Fine-grade steel wool
- Acrylic primer
- Fine-grade sandpaper
- Household paintbrush
- Satin finish water-based paint
- Fabric

A

1 CAREFULLY STRIP THE ORIGINAL FABRIC COVERING AND the underlying layers of padding off the frame or bring to an upholsterer and have him or her remove all the materials. If you want to strip the frame yourself, consult a good book on upholstery techniques (see Resources, pages 155–56). [photo A]

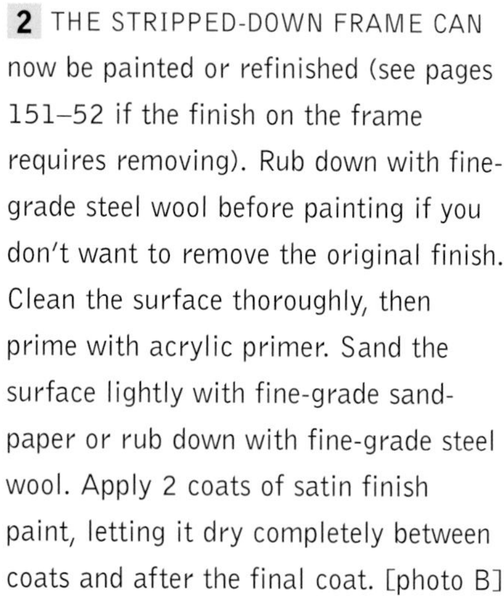

2 THE STRIPPED-DOWN FRAME CAN now be painted or refinished (see pages 151–52 if the finish on the frame requires removing). Rub down with fine-grade steel wool before painting if you don't want to remove the original finish. Clean the surface thoroughly, then prime with acrylic primer. Sand the surface lightly with fine-grade sandpaper or rub down with fine-grade steel wool. Apply 2 coats of satin finish paint, letting it dry completely between coats and after the final coat. [photo B]

B

3 THE CHAIR IS NOW READY TO BE re-covered with the new fabric. If you are doing this yourself, again, use a good reference book on upholstery. If you are working with an upholsterer, bring the chair to the shop after it is painted and completely dry along with all the materials and layers of padding that have been previously removed.

C

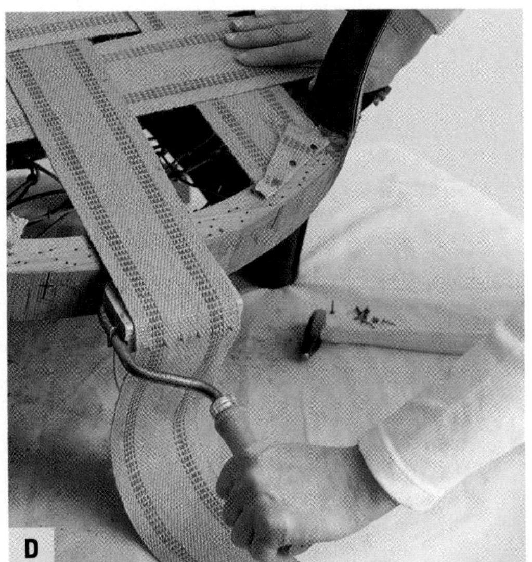
D

E

new life for sprung upholstered pieces

The lovely, slightly faded green velvet on this chair was still in good condition but the webbing under the seat had completely given out and the springs underneath needed to be retied and attached to the frame. Rather than completely reupholster the piece I decided to dismantle the chair just enough to reach the springs and repair them. To gain access to the springs I needed first to completely remove the covering and padding on the lower part of the chair. Here's how to do it yourself: Using the end of a screwdriver, tap against the tacks to loosen them; you'll then be able to pull the tacks out with pliers. Working slowly, remove all of the old covering and padding with care, preserving everything for later reuse. [photo C]

After the lower part of the frame is completely stripped the new webbing can be stretched across the underside of the seat using a webbing stretcher, which creates the necessary tension. Start by placing the free end of the new webbing over the frame so that the end extends about an inch beyond the frame. Tack the webbing to the frame with four tacks. Fold the short end back on itself and tack again through both layers in three places. Using the stretcher, stretch the webbing across the frame, hold it down and attach it to the other side of the frame with four tacks. Trim the end allowing an inch beyond the tacks; fold the end back on itself. Follow the spacing of the original webbing and repeat the process from back to front across the frame and then from one side to the other side weaving the webbing over and under the vertical pieces as you go. [photo D]

With the firm base of the new webbing in place the springs are now ready to be retied. [photo E]

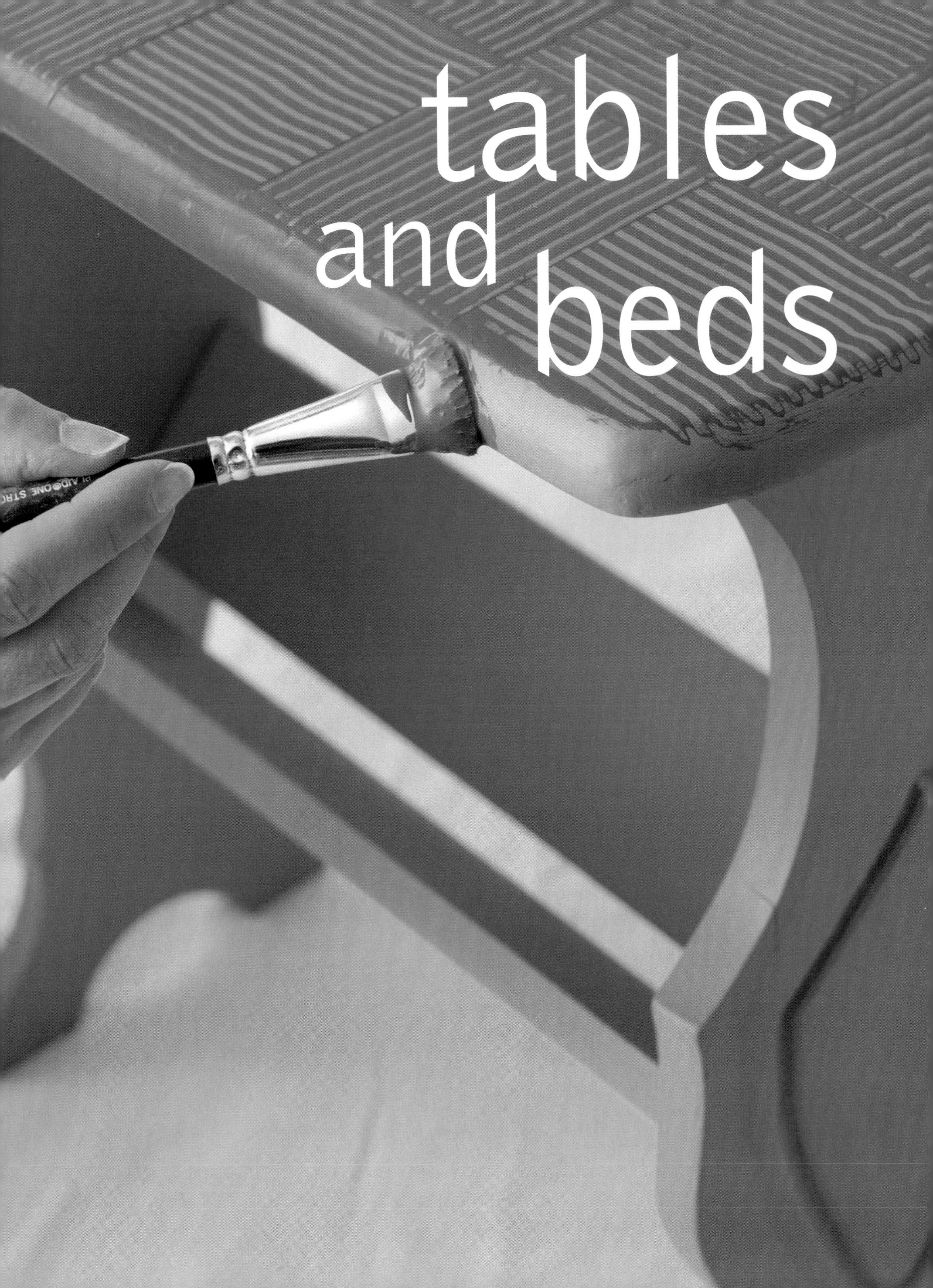

tables and beds

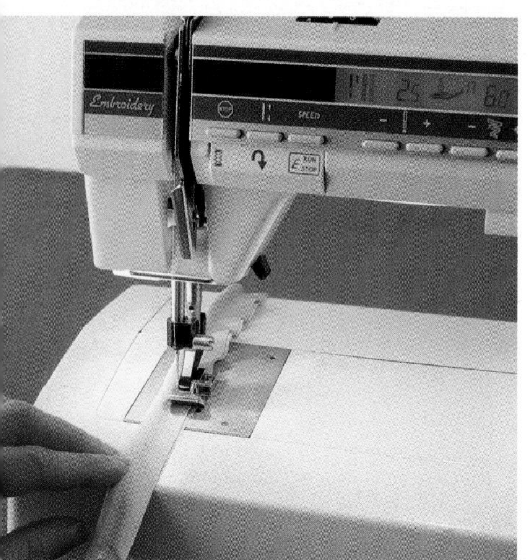

while we all respond to the

desire for a luxurious bedroom, we don't always know how to achieve it for ourselves. Nothing makes the bedroom feel more indulgent than the centerpiece of the room, the bed. If you have inherited a wonderful antique canopy bed, or have the means to acquire one, it's fairly easy to create a sense of warm glamour. But for those of us without the luck or the means, there are other less traditional ways of attaining a haven of personal luxury and comfort. Instead of a more traditional bed, you can marry two disparate pieces as I did here to create something luxurious but affordable. The battered dinette bench and grand-scale but cracked Eastlake-style headboard fit effortlessly together to secure what I've always wanted—a serene and comfortable private retreat for rest and relaxation. The beautiful Fortuny cotton fabric on the insert in the headboard and the bench cushion come from my grandmother Carrie, the woman who first taught me to sew and appreciate the luxury of good fabric. When I climb into this bed now I am reminded of her and enveloped in the gently faded, antique fabric she gave me.

Custom-made upholstered headboards are quite expensive to have made but lots of older bed frames like this one are ideal substitutes. Look especially for ones with a center panel section that can be used to position the fabric-covered padded insert. If you fall in love with a headboard without a center panel, you can still have the delight of a wonderful textile in the bedroom by making a fabric slipcover to fit over both the head- and footboard. It will change the look and feel of the frame dramatically and can completely update a room. The bench was a fortuitous idea and I like it even better than a regular footboard because it serves as a very useful temporary storage space.

Another economical but striking alternative is to take an unusual piece like the mirrored panel and make it serve as a headboard—pile pillows covered in antique lace and soft colors in front to create a cozy and comfortably sensuous bed. Look for other opportunities for unexpected pairs, like a simple headboard and a low rectangular upholstered bench, and tie the pieces together with fabric and paint.

Small tables are another element I've used time and time again—they function both as useful surfaces and decorative touches. They can be especially useful when entertaining—as a second bar area or an additional surface for hors d'oeuvres. Use the top of a small table to show off a collection or improvise a work area in front of a sunny window. The top of a smallish table provides a neat flat surface for bringing a bold splash of color or pattern and providing instant personality for the piece. And if the table is a small one it will not dominate the setting but enliven the surrounding space. Now is the time to take a chance with a favorite quirky color or the brilliant shine of metal to turn these odd small pieces into special treasures that add individual charm to your home. This is a chance to experiment with the unusual; you can always change it the next year when you tire of the splashy purple or metallic squares.

Console Table

I'D ALWAYS WANTED A TABLE IN MY DINING ROOM TO PROVIDE SOME EXTRA SERVING SPACE. BUT I REVISED MY IDEA WHEN I CAME ACROSS THESE LARGE, ORNATELY CARVED BRACKETS. THEY APPEAR TO BE SUPPORTING THE TABLE BUT IN REALITY THE PIECE IS HUNG ON THE WALL AS ONE UNIT. THE TOP IS MADE FROM NEW BIRCH PLYWOOD AND THE WIDE CARVED MOLDING IS THE TYPE USED ON MANTELPIECES. I PAINTED AN OLD MIRROR TO MATCH AND HUNG IT JUST ABOVE THE SHELF SURFACE AT EYE LEVEL. BUT I THINK IT WOULD LOOK JUST AS GOOD WITH A FRAMED PICTURE AND TWO SCONCES HANGING ON EITHER SIDE OF THE PICTURE. BRACKETS LIKE THOSE SHOWN HERE ARE OFTEN AVAILABLE FROM STORES THAT SPECIALIZE IN ARCHITECTURAL SALVAGE. YOU MAY BE ABLE TO FIND SOMETHING LESS ORNATE BUT SIMILAR AT A BUILDING SUPPLY STORE.

materials

Wood brackets	Clamp
½-inch plywood with birch veneered face	Hammer
Miter box with saw (optional)	Wood putty
4-inch-wide bolection or mantel molding	Small weights
Wood glue	Fine-grade sandpaper
Finishing nails	Acrylic primer
	Satin finish water-based paint
	3- and 4-inch wood screws

1 THE TOP OF THIS TABLE MEASURES 13 X 38 INCHES. THESE measurements can be adjusted to fit the depth of your brackets and the width of your space. The depth of the top does not have to match the depth of the brackets exactly and can be adjusted to fit your needs and space considerations. After you decide on the size of your top, cut 2 pieces of plywood to those measurements. Cut 3 pieces of the molding, 1 for the front edge and 2 for the sides, to those measurements, mitering both corners on the front piece and only one corner on the side pieces, and cutting the other end straight across. The lumberyard should be able to cut these pieces as well as the plywood for you. [photo A]

2 MAKE A BOX THAT IS OPEN IN the back by attaching the molding to the plywood bottom and top. Glue the side pieces of the molding in place along the lower and top edges of the plywood with the wood glue. Secure the molding further with finishing nails. Cut 2 pieces of scrap plywood to fit inside the box, gluing each one vertically on the inside between the top and bottom pieces to provide some additional support for the top. Clamp the molding to hold it in place until the glue sets. Glue the front piece of molding in place along the

A

B

top and bottom edges, making sure to use plenty of glue at the 2 mitered corners. Wipe any excess glue away with a damp cloth or paper towel. Clamp until the glue sets. Secure the molding further with finishing nails. Recess all the nails using a punch or another nail.

3 FILL ANY SPACES OR GAPS ALONG the edges or nail holes in the molding with wood putty. Place the top, face-side down, on a smooth surface and mark the position of the brackets, placing them 6 to 8 inches in from the sides. Glue the brackets to the underside of the top with the wood glue. Clamp or place weights on the brackets until the glue sets and is completely dry. Sand the piece lightly and prime everything, including the brackets, with the acrylic primer. Paint with 2 coats of the satin finish water-based paint, letting the paint dry between coats. Let dry completely. [photo B]

4 TO HANG THE UNIT ON THE WALL, ATTACH 2 SMALL BLOCKS of wood to the wall at the desired height (I hung this at counter height, 36 inches from the floor to the top). The blocks should be narrow enough so that the opening in the back of the table is able to slip over them but deep enough to provide support to the table, which will rest on top of the blocks: I used two 4-inch lengths of a 2×4. Anchor the blocks firmly into the wall beams with 4-inch-long wood screws so they can support the weight of the table. Slip the unit over the blocks and drill holes downward through the tabletop into each block in 2 places. Screw into place with 3-inch-long wood screws. Recess the screw heads and fill the holes with wood putty. If there is a large gap between the table and the wall it can be filled in with caulk and painted to match.

choosing stock moldings

Many different kinds, sizes, and shapes of stock moldings are available. For the best selection seek out the stores or catalogs that offer specialty moldings—you will find a wider and more interesting range to choose from. Moldings can be used individually as here, or stacked one on top of another to produce a more elaborate effect. Visit a historical home or period room in a museum to see how moldings are used in the mantels and fireplace surrounds, for chair or picture rails, or to create detailing on doors and embellish windows.

Carved Mirrored Panel

WHEN WE BOUGHT OUR HOUSE IN THE COUNTRY A FEW YEARS AGO, MY FATHER GAVE ME THIS OLD CARVED WOOD PANEL. IT ORIGINALLY CAME FROM AN UPRIGHT PIANO AND FORMED THE FRONT SECTION WHERE THE SHEET MUSIC RESTED. SOMETIME LATER, I NOTICED A PHOTO IN A MAGAZINE OF A MIRRORED AND CARVED PANEL HANGING OVER A BED, SERVING AS THE HEADBOARD. I IMMEDIATELY THOUGHT ABOUT THE PIANO PANEL. AND EVEN THOUGH THE PANEL NOW LOOKS VERY DIFFERENT FROM MY ORIGINAL INSPIRATION, IN THE END, IT SUITS MY NEEDS AND THE STYLE OF THIS BEDROOM PERFECTLY.

IF YOU CAN'T FIND SUCH A LARGE PIECE, YOU CAN ASSEMBLE A SIMILAR ONE BY USING A SELECTION OF DECORATIVE MOLDINGS AND CARVED WOOD ORNAMENTS, EITHER OLD OR NEW, TO RE-CREATE THE LOOK. JUST BUILD UP THE LAYERS IN A SIMILAR FASHION USING A RECTANGULAR PIECE OF VENEERED PLYWOOD OR AN OLD SHUTTER AS A BASE AND PAINT, ADDING A MIRROR TO THE CENTER PANEL. IT COULD ALSO BE VERY EFFECTIVE WITH A MIRROR IN EACH OF THE THREE PANELS.

materials

Wood panel	Cheesecloth
Sandpaper	Beveled-edge mirror
Acrylic primer	Mirror adhesive
Pale color satin finish water-based paint	Awl
White water-based paint	Hangers/screws
Large household paintbrush	Heavy-duty picture wire
	Rubber bumpers

1 SAND THE PANEL LIGHTLY AND PRIME THE whole piece, including the moldings, with the acrylic primer. Paint with 2 coats of the pale satin finish water-based paint, letting it dry between coats. Let dry completely. To bring out the details of the carving, make a wash by diluting 1 part white water-based paint with 8 parts water. With the large paintbrush, lightly and quickly brush out the wash, letting it puddle a little in the carved-out areas. [photo A]

A

2 USING A PAD OF CHEESECLOTH, DAB AT THE wash to soften it. Then wipe off most of the wash from the highlights of the moldings and the flat surfaces of the panel, leaving some remaining in the recesses. Let dry completely. [photo B]

B

3 MEASURE THE CENTER PANEL OPENING AND have a beveled-edge mirror cut to fit. Glue the mirror into the opening with mirror adhesive following the manufacturer's directions. [photo C]

4 USING AN AWL, MARK THE PLACEMENT FOR THE hangers about one third down from the upper edge on each side. Screw the hangers onto the back of the panel. Thread heavy-duty picture wire 3 or 4 times through one hanger, twisting the end back on itself. Stretch the wire across the back to the opposite side and thread through the second hanger as before, allowing enough slack so the wire falls about 2 to 3 inches from the top of the panel when hung. Secure rubber bumpers to the back lower corners of the panel.

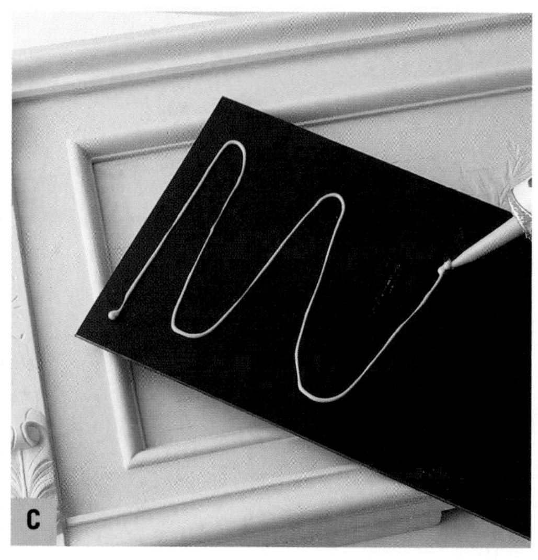
C

5 HANG THE PANEL FROM TWO HEAVY-DUTY SCREWS FIRMLY anchored into the studs behind the wall. Two separate hangers spaced on either side of the center point will work to distribute the weight evenly, so the panel will hang straighter and more securely. Think carefully about the correct height when you hang the panel. The lower edge should be positioned just high enough so that your head will not bump into it when you are sitting up in bed. You could also attach it directly to the bed frame by screwing 2×4′s (painted to match) onto the back of the panel and attaching them to the bed frame.

replacing and moving the molding

If the piece is missing any molding, it can be replaced, or perhaps resituated from another section. Measure the space and cut a piece of the matching molding to replace the missing section. Alternatively, remove a piece of unneeded molding and reposition it, as I did here in the center section. I also needed to add new molding to the lower edge of the right outside panel, where it was missing. Because the size of the new molding was slightly different than the original I decided to replace the piece of original molding on the left with new molding so that both of the outside lower edges would match. Add a piece of wood underneath if necessary to provide a surface for the extra molding to sit on. Glue in place first before attaching the molding. Glue the new piece of molding and any recycled piece of molding in place with the wood glue. Clamp or place weights on the molding until the glue sets and is completely dry. [photo D]

D

Combed Table

SMALL ODD TABLES LIKE THIS ARE A STYLISH ALTERNATIVE TO A COFFEE TABLE. YOU CAN GROUP TWO OR THREE TOGETHER FOR A LARGER SURFACE AREA OR SCATTER THEM AROUND A ROOM. THEY DON'T TAKE UP VERY MUCH SPACE AND ARE LIGHT ENOUGH TO BE MOVED FREQUENTLY. THEIR SCALE MAKES THEM THE PERFECT COMPANION FOR A SMALL COUCH LIKE THE ONE HERE OR IN A SMALLER ROOM WHERE SPACE IS LIMITED. THEY ARE FAIRLY EASY TO FIND AT FLEA MARKETS OR HOUSE SALES. I FOUND THIS ONE AT A SMALL FLEA MARKET IN UPSTATE NEW YORK. IN THIS ROOM IT NEEDED TO BE PAINTED A STRONG COLOR TO STAND UP TO THE FLORAL PATTERN ON THE COUCH, BUT I'VE SEEN A SIMILAR TABLE PAINTED ANTIQUE WHITE AND IT LOOKED EQUALLY NICE.

materials

- Small wooden table
- Sandpaper
- Lighter color satin finish water-based paint
- Small foam paint roller
- Colored pencil to match deeper shade paint
- Ruler
- Painter's tape
- Craft knife
- Water-based glaze medium
- Concentrated artist's acrylic paint in deeper shade
- Small household paintbrush
- Combing tool
- Artist's brush
- Matte finish varnish

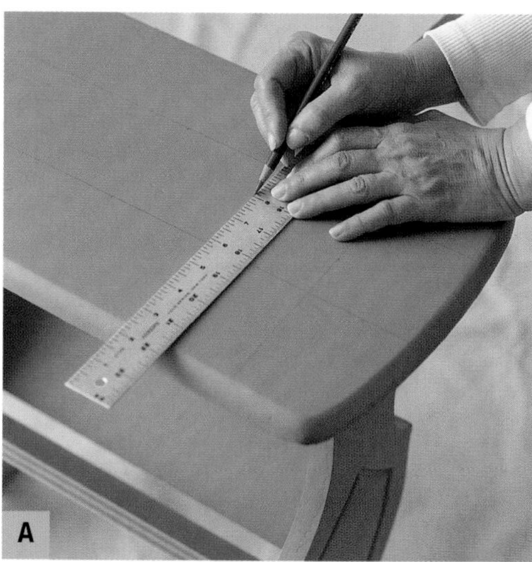

A

1 SAND THE TABLE AS MUCH AS NECESSARY TO ACHIEVE A smooth surface and remove any old, flaking paint. Paint with 2 coats (letting dry between coats) of the satin finish water-based paint. Let dry completely. Using the colored pencil and the ruler, divide the tabletop into 3-inch squares, marking them lightly on the surface of the table. [photo A]

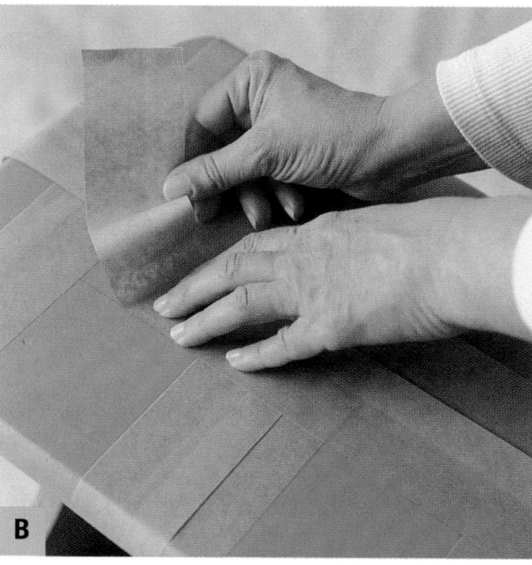

B

2 USING THE PAINTER'S TAPE, MARK OFF ROWS OF ALTERNATE squares. These squares will be painted and combed first. [photo B]

3 MIX ONE PART GLAZE MEDIUM WITH ONE PART OF THE artist's acrylic paint. For the horizontal squares, use the small paintbrush to apply the tinted glaze with even, horizontal brush strokes to one square at a time. [photo C]

C

E

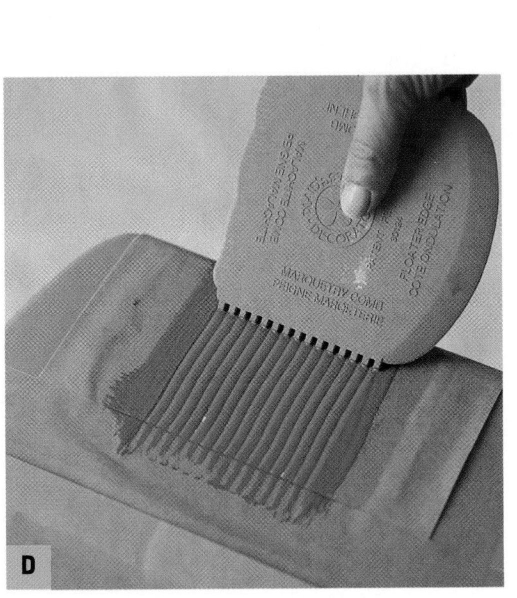

D

4 STARTING AT THE LEFT EDGE, DRAG THE COMB FROM LEFT TO right through the tinted glaze. For even lines, drag the comb in one fluid movement. If the glaze smudges, smooth out with the paint-brush and a little more of the tinted glaze and try again. Wipe the combing tool after each square to remove excess glaze. [photo D]

5 LET THE SQUARES DRY COMPLETELY AND THEN REMOVE THE tape. [photo E]

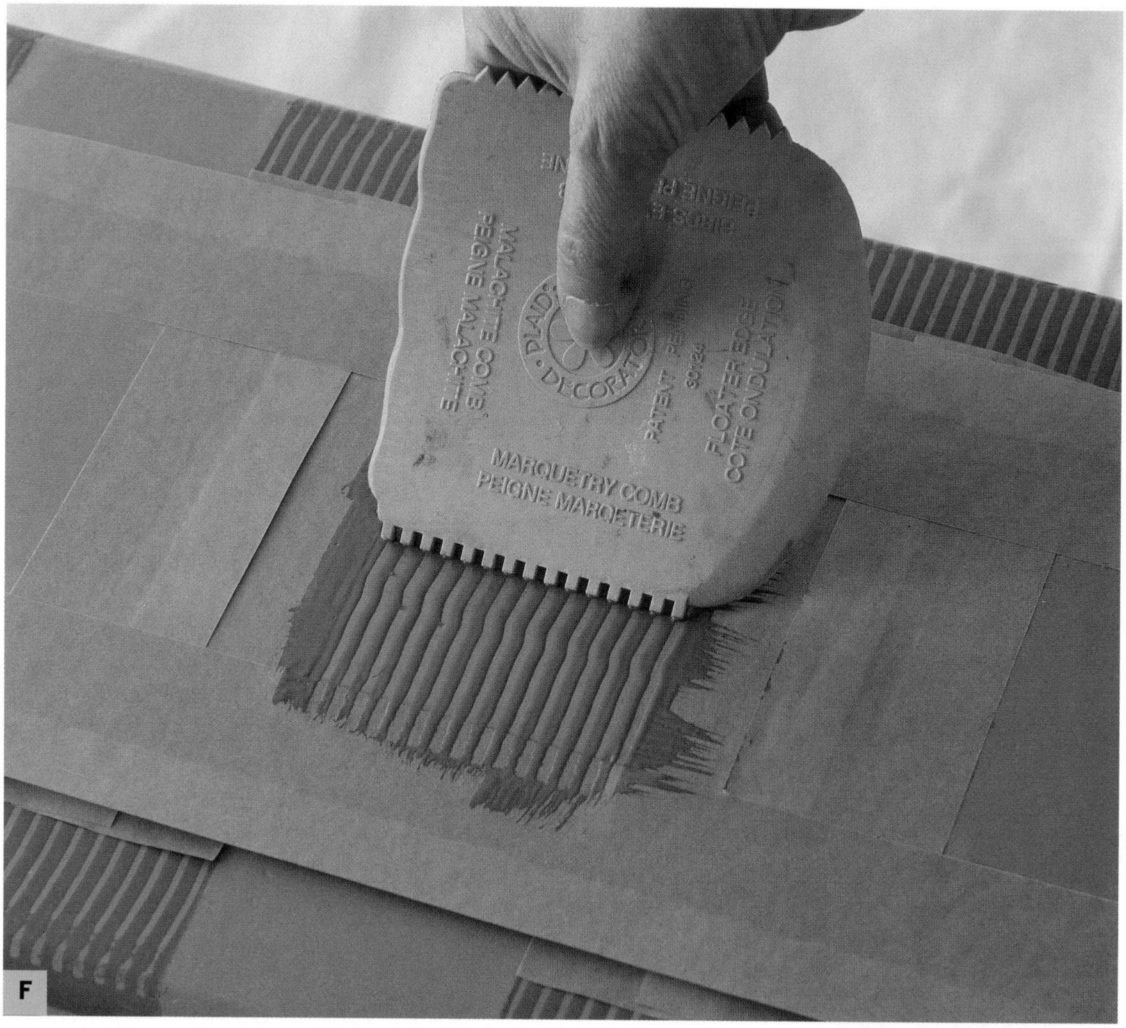

F

6 REPEAT THE TAPING, PAINTING, AND COMBING FOR ALTERnate rows of horizontal squares. [photo F]

7 WHEN COMPLETELY DRY, REMOVE THE OLD TAPE AND USING the painter's tape, mark off the vertical squares that do not touch along alternate rows. Working on one square at a time as before, apply the glaze with even vertical brush strokes, but this time start at the top of the square and drag the comb down to the bottom. Let dry completely and then remove the tape. Repeat the process for the remaining vertical squares. [photo G]

G

8 USING THE ARTIST'S PAINTBRUSH AND THE TINTED GLAZE, hand paint the edge of the table to give it a finished look. Let dry. Apply 2 coats of matte varnish to the tabletop to finish. [photo H]

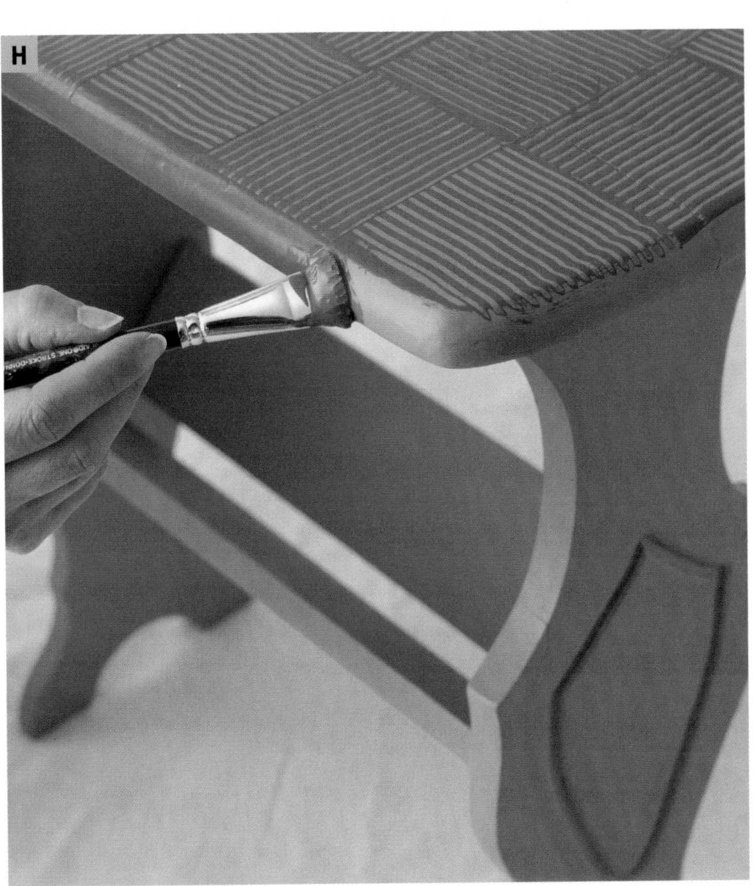

H

how to make a combing tool

Different-sized combing tools can be purchased, but they are easy to make yourself to suit the scale of your project. For a larger project, grooves can be cut in a window washer's squeegee with a craft knife. A piece of sturdy cardboard works well as a temporary combing tool for a smaller project. It will wear out more quickly than a rubber one, so plan your use accordingly. Experiment with the size and spacing of the grooves until you are satisfied with the results.

alternate color combinations

Padded Headboard

WE HAD BEEN USING THIS EASTLAKE-STYLE HEADBOARD FOR A WHILE WHEN IT DEVELOPED A LARGE CRACK THAT COULD NOT BE REPAIRED. I WAS LOATH TO PART WITH IT, SO I DECIDED TO COVER THE AREA WITH A PADDED FABRIC INSERT. THIS SIMPLE TECHNIQUE CAN WORK WITH A VARIETY OF HEADBOARDS AS WELL. MANY LARGE THRIFT SHOPS HAVE A PLENTIFUL SUPPLY OF OLD BED FRAMES. IF YOU CAN'T FIND A HEADBOARD AND FOOTBOARD TO MATCH, USE A HIGH-BACKED BENCH PAINTED TO MATCH THE HEADBOARD AT THE FOOT OF THE BED AS I DID HERE TO CREATE THE ILLUSION OF A MATCHING SET.

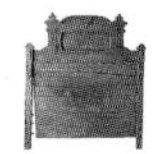

materials

Headboard
Wood glue
Small wood block
Hammer
Sandpaper
Satin finish oil-based paint
Household paintbrush
Small paint roller

PADDED INSERT

Ruler
Scissors
¼-inch-thick medium-density fiberboard
Cotton fabric
Polyester batting
High-density foam
Soft lead pencil
Staples/staple gun
2-inch-wide Velcro adhesive-back tape

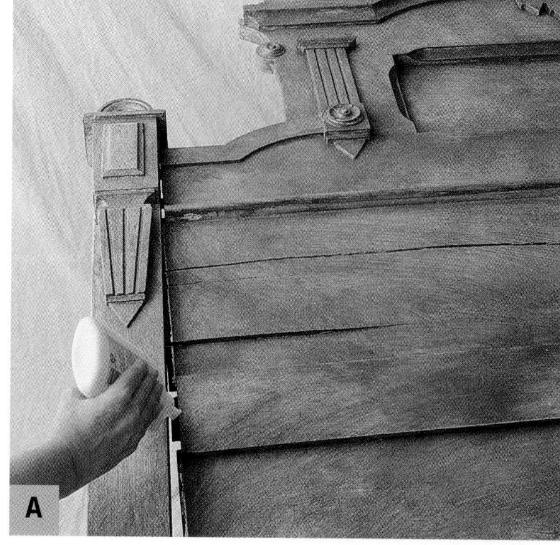

A

1 INSPECT THE HEADBOARD FOR ANY LOOSE JOINTS. REATTACH if necessary, using wood glue. [photo A]

2 USING A WOOD BLOCK TO PROTECT THE SURFACE FROM dents, bang any loose parts, such as legs, back into place using a hammer. Let the glue dry completely. [photo B]

B

3 SAND THE ENTIRE SURFACE LIGHTLY. PAINT THE HEADboard with 2 coats of satin finish oil-based paint. Let dry completely between each coat and after the final coat.

4 MEASURE THE AREA ON THE HEADBOARD WHERE THE padded insert will go. Cut a piece of ¼-inch-thick fiberboard to fit the area. Place the board on top of the fabric, centering any motifs carefully, and mark the outline on the wrong side. Add at least 4 inches all around for wrapping and stretching the fabric around the board, then cut out the fabric.

5 CUT 2 PIECES OF POLYESTER BATTING, ONE the same size as the fiberboard and one 1 inch smaller all around. Cut one piece of foam 1 inch smaller all around. Place the fabric, right-side down, on a work surface. Center the 2 pieces of batting, then the foam, on the fabric, using your markings as a guide, with the smaller piece on top, then the foam, and then the board. [photo C]

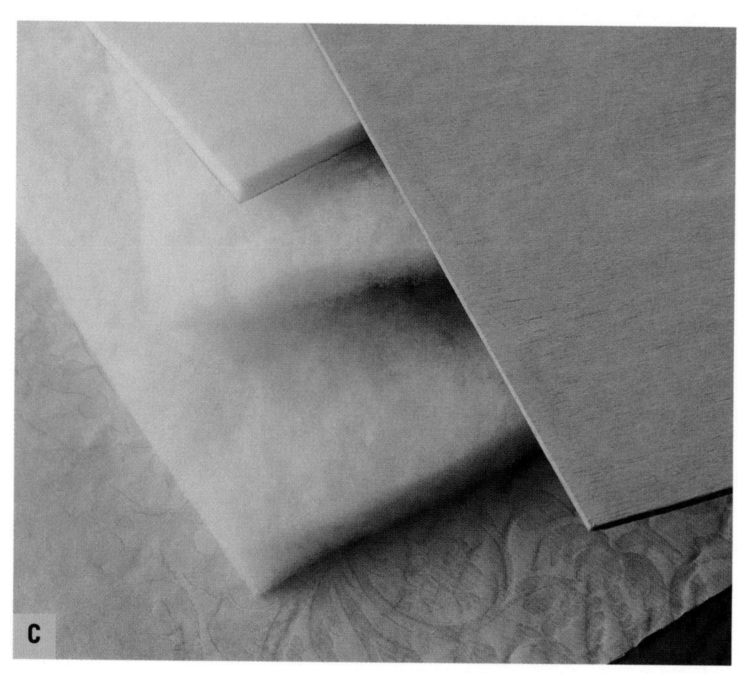

C

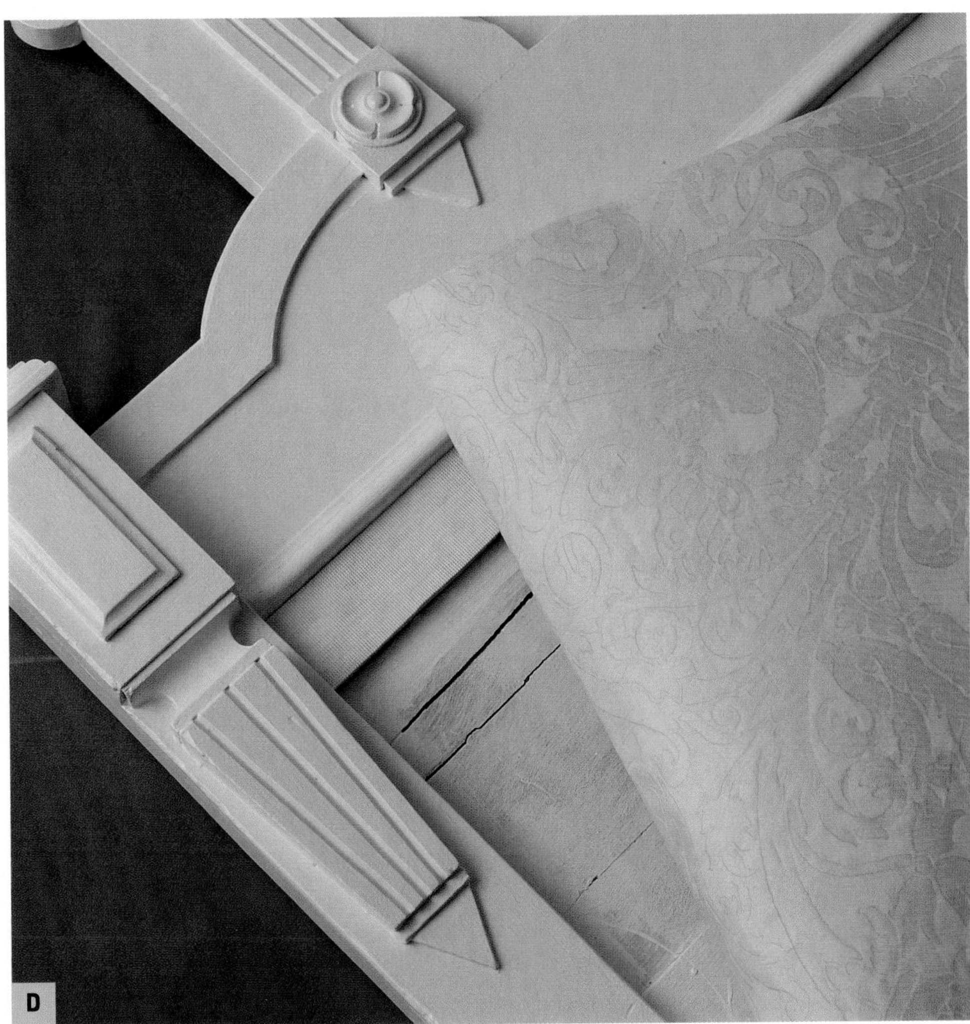

D

6 ALIGN THE GRAIN OF THE FABRIC WITH THE EDGE OF THE board, wrap the excess fabric to the back of the board, pulling firmly, and staple in place. Complete one side at a time, starting in the center and working out toward the corners. Fold in excess fabric at the corners and staple in place.

7 SECURE THE NONHOOK SIDE OF THE VELCRO TAPE TO THE padded insert along the top and bottom edges on the back side of the panel by stapling in place (or pressing in place if it has an adhesive backing). Secure the hook side of the Velcro tape to the top and bottom edges of the opening on the headboard where the padded fabric insert will go. Position the padded panel in the headboard opening and press into place. [photo D]

Wooden Bench

USED IN DINETTE AREAS IN THE FIFTIES, THIS OLD KITCHEN BENCH HAS FOUND A COMPLETELY NEW PURPOSE IN THE BEDROOM. YOU CAN USE THESE BENCHES AT THE FOOT OF A BED TO SUBSTITUTE FOR THE FOOTBOARD AND CREATE A SENSE OF ENCLOSURE. THE BENCH WILL KEEP THE DRAFTS OFF YOUR FEET, BE A HANGER FOR YOUR ROBE, AND PROVIDE A PLACE TO STACK UP THOSE EXTRA PILLOWS. SHOES OR A LAUNDRY BASKET CAN BE STORED, OUT OF THE WAY, UNDERNEATH.

materials

Bench
Sandpaper
Acrylic primer
Wood putty
Putty knife
Satin finish oil-based paint
Household paintbrush
Small paint roller

CUSHION

Brown paper
Soft lead pencil
Ruler
Scissors
Cotton fabric for cushion covers
Accent fabric for piping and buttons
Cotton cording for piping
Sewing machine
Hand sewing needle
Cotton sewing thread to match fabric
Iron

FOR FABRIC-COVERED BUTTONS (OPTIONAL)

Hand sewing needle
Cotton thread
1-inch plastic curtain rings
Silk embroidery thread
Hand embroidery needle

NEW CUSHION PAD (OPTIONAL)

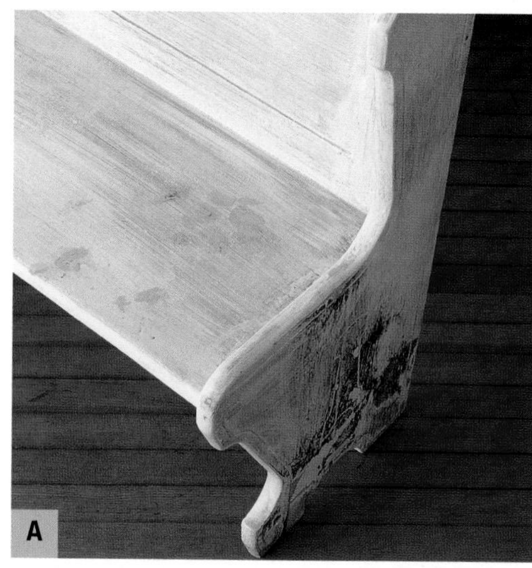

A

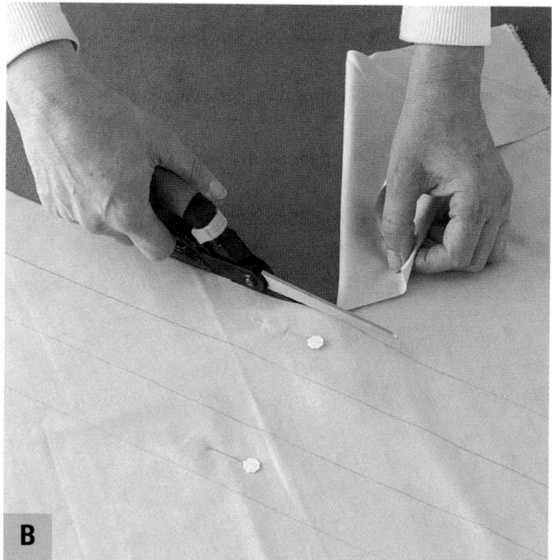

B

1 SAND THE BENCH AS MUCH AS NECESSARY TO REMOVE THE gloss from the paint surface. If it is a dark color, prime with the acrylic primer; otherwise just proceed without priming. Apply wood putty over any chips, cracks, or other blemishes on the surface. Deeper holes might need more than one application of putty. Push the putty down into the cracks with the putty knife. Draw the knife across the surface, smoothing the excess putty as you go. Let the putty dry until hard. Sand the surface lightly with fine-grade sandpaper. Paint with 2 coats of satin finish oil-based paint. Let dry completely between each coat and after the final coat. [photo A]

2 MAKE A PAPER PATTERN THE EXACT SIZE OF THE BENCH seat, adding a ½-inch seam allowance all around. Use the pattern to cut out the cushion top and bottom from the cotton fabric. Using the method on pages 58–59, cut enough 1½-inch bias strips from the accent fabric to pipe around the seat cushion. [photo B]

3 TO JOIN THE BIAS STRIPS TOGETHER, CUT THE ENDS AT A right angle and overlap the 2 ends' right sides together at right (90°) angles to each other. Machine stitch across the diagonal, trim off the corner, and press open. Repeat with the other strips. Lay the cord in the center of the wrong side of the bias strip and fold in half. Using a zipper foot, machine stitch as close to the cord as possible. [photo C]

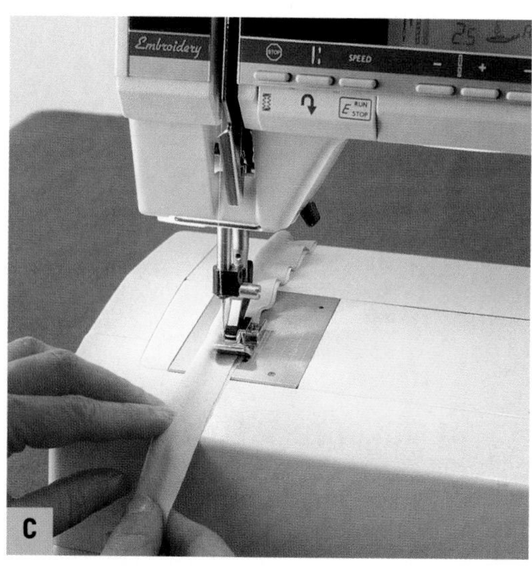

C

fabric-covered buttons using plastic rings

Use a small circular object or make a template out of thin cardboard for a pattern. Fabric circles should measure about twice the diameter of the ring: For example, a $\frac{3}{4}$-inch-wide ring will need a $1\frac{1}{2}$-inch-wide circle of fabric. Trace the circles and cut out. With a needle and a doubled and knotted piece of thread, use a running stitch to sew around the edge of one of the circles of fabric. The fabric will gather and start to form a pouch. Place a plastic ring in the center of the fabric pouch and pull on the thread to close the opening. Anchor the gathered fabric in place by sewing the fabric circle closed on the underside using the same thread and needle. Finish by knotting and cutting the thread. With silk embroidery thread, make very small decorative running stitches around the inside edge of the ring, working on the top side of the button. Repeat to make as many buttons as needed. [photo E]

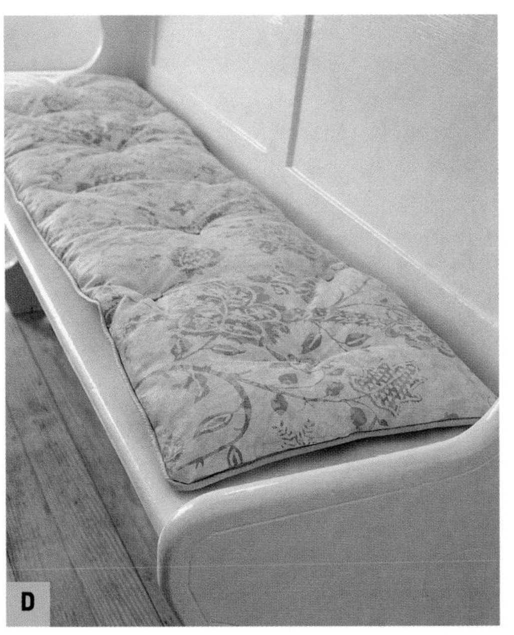

D

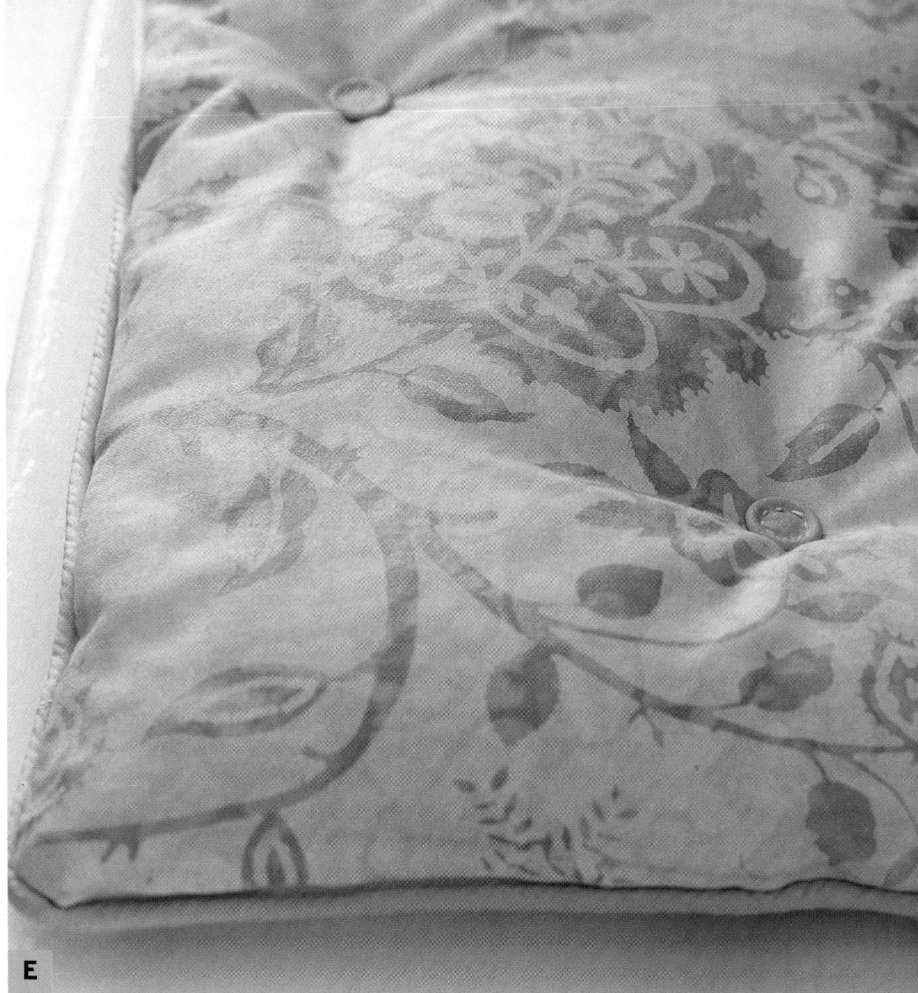

E

4 WITH THE RAW EDGES TOGETHER, PIN THE PIPING TO THE right side of the top cushion cover fabric and machine stitch, allowing a $\frac{1}{2}$-inch seam allowance. Snip the piping seam allowance when turning the corners to allow the piping to lay flat. Lay the bottom cushion fabric underneath, with the right sides together, and machine stitch following the previous stitching line, leaving an opening on one long side to insert the pad. Trim the fabric at the corners, turn right-side out, and press. Insert the new pad into the cushion cover and hand-sew the opening closed using a needle and cotton thread to match. To make your own cushion pad, please see directions page 152.

5 IF DESIRED, PAIRS OF BUTTONS CAN BE SEWN ONTO THE TOP and bottom of the pad with an extra-long needle. Thread the needle with an extra-long piece of heavy-duty thread and make a single stitch to hold the buttons in place. Insert the needle completely through the cushion to the underside and back up again through the top, attaching the buttons. Pull the thread taut to make the dimpled effect and tie very securely. Cut the threads and hide the ends underneath the button. [photo D]

Metal Leg Table

THIS WELL-WEATHERED LOW TABLE HAD SPENT MANY SEASONS OUTDOORS AND WAS SHOWING THE EFFECT OF THE ELEMENTS: THE TOP WAS PEELING AND THE LEGS RUSTING. CLEANING AND STRIPPING THE LEGS DOWN TO BARE SHINING METAL INSPIRED ME TO USE A SILVER-COLORED METALLIC LEAF TO DECORATE THE TOP. IF YOU USE ALUMINUM LEAF, WHICH IS EASIER TO FIND AND LESS EXPENSIVE THAN REAL SILVER LEAF, THE SURFACE WON'T TARNISH THE WAY SILVER DOES AND IT LOOKS JUST AS NICE. I LIKE THE SIMPLE REPETITION OF THE SQUARE SHAPES AS THEY ECHO THE SQUARE SURFACE OF THE TOP. OUTDOORS ON A WARM DAY, THE SUN BOUNCES AND SHIMMERS ACROSS THE METAL LEAF.

SMALL PATCHES OF METAL LEAF CAN BE USED TO BRIGHTEN UP OTHER OBJECTS: A LAMP SHADE, A PICTURE FRAME, OR EVEN A SMALL TRAY COULD BE TREATED TO SOME METALLIC FLASH.

materials

- Folding table with metal legs
- Paint remover
- Steel wool
- Power drill with wire brush attachment
- Spray lacquer
- Power sander or sandpaper
- Wood putty
- Acrylic primer
- Eggshell finish water-based paint
- Household iron
- Iron-on wood veneer edging
- Craft knife
- Small foam roller
- White Conte pencil
- Ruler
- Painter's tape or masking tape
- Basic gilding kit: gilding size, book of aluminum leaf, natural-hair brush, cheesecloth
- Single-edge razor blade
- Matte finish varnish
- Brush for varnish
- $\frac{1}{4}$-inch-thick clear glass cut to fit tabletop

1 STRIP ANY PAINT OFF THE METAL LEGS WITH PAINT remover following the manufacturer's directions. When the paint is completely removed, the legs can be further polished using steel wool or can be given a brushed-steel finish by using a power drill with a wire brush attachment. When you have achieved the desired result, spray legs with lacquer to protect the finish.

2 SAND THE TABLETOP UNTIL SMOOTH OR, IF NECESSARY, peel off the top layer of plywood, then sand; any uneven spots still remaining on the top can be filled with wood putty. Sand again if necessary, then prime with the acrylic primer. Sand lightly again and paint with 2 coats of eggshell finish water-based paint. Let dry completely between each coat and after the final coat. Using a household iron, iron the wood veneer edging onto the outside rim of the tabletop. Any excess can easily be trimmed off afterward using the craft knife. Sand the veneer edging lightly, prime, and paint as above. [photo A]

3 USING THE WHITE CONTE PENCIL AND THE RULER, MEASURE and mark 1-inch squares on the tabletop. First draw parallel vertical lines for the sides of each square starting from the center of the table and working out to each side, then draw parallel horizontal lines to complete each square. Mark the center of each of the squares to be gilded lightly with an X. [photo B]

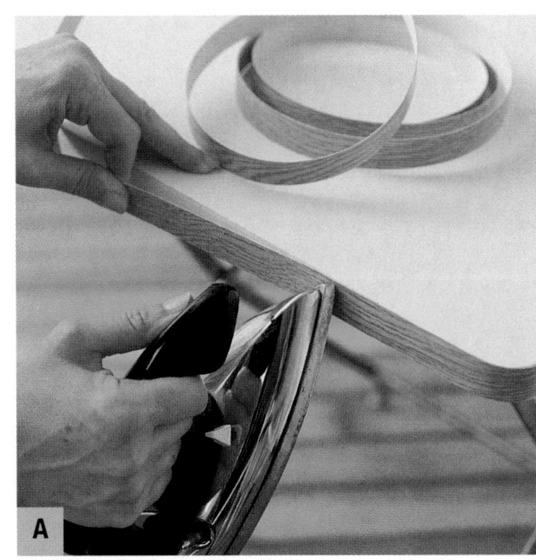

A

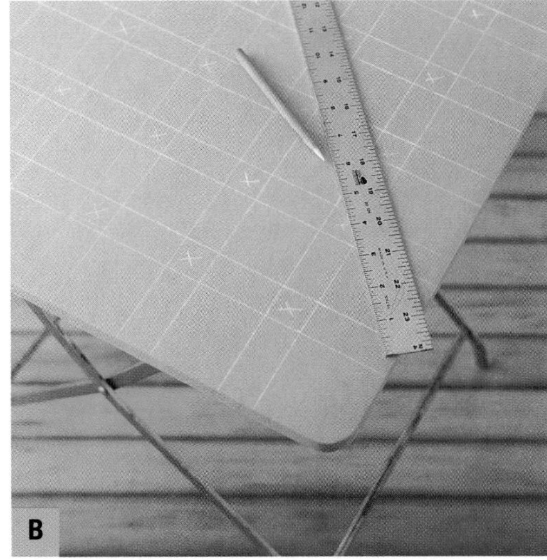

B

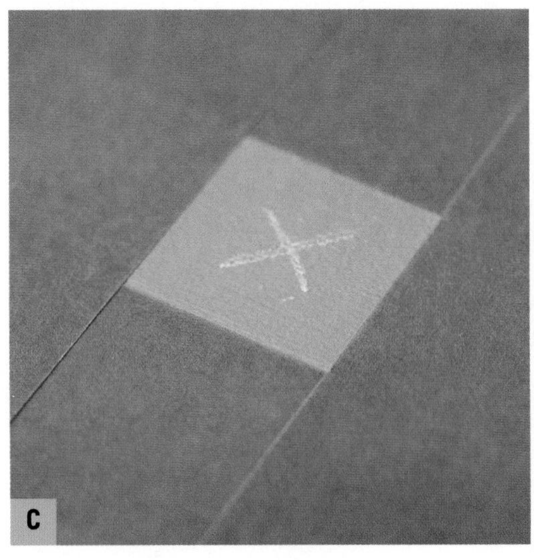

C

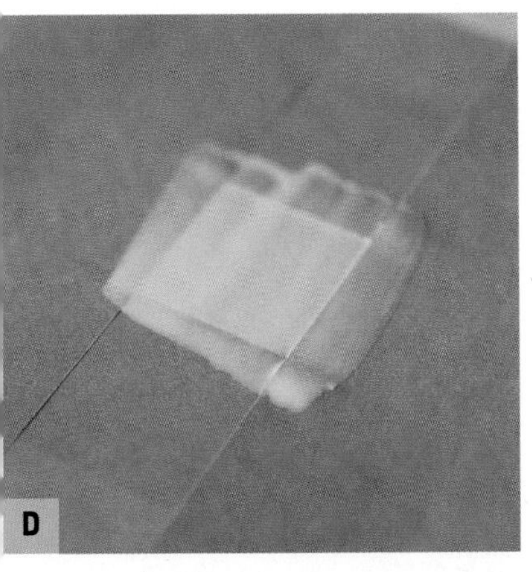

D

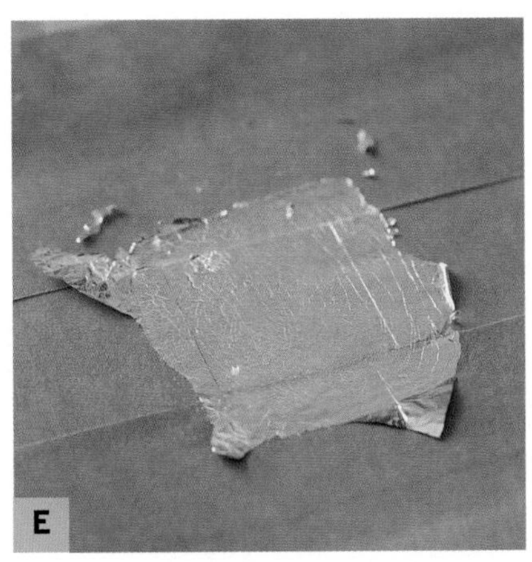

E

F

tips for working with metal leaf

The size is ready to receive the leaf when it is almost dry but still tacky. This size became less opaque and more clear as it dried, an indication that it was reaching the right degree of tackiness. Different types of size will have different drying times and characteristics—for the best results make sure to read and follow the manufacturer's instructions carefully. Handle the leaf gently—it is very fragile. Wear thin cotton gloves or dust your fingers with talcum powder to keep the natural oils on your fingers off of the metal leaf (which becomes discolored from the contact).

4 USE THE PAINTER'S TAPE OR MASKING TAPE TO MARK OFF each of the squares to be gilded. If they are too close together it might be necessary to work on alternate squares and repeat. [photo C]

5 GILD THE SQUARES, FOLLOWING THE INSTRUCTIONS IN THE gilding kit. Pay special attention to applying the size. The layer of size should be flowed onto the area to be gilded very evenly and as smoothly as possible. It needs to be as even and as thin as possible so that all the areas to be gilded will be ready at the same time. Apply only one even coat and do not overbrush. [photo D]

6 WHEN THE SIZE HAS REACHED TACK, APPLY THE ALUMINUM leaf, following the instructions in the gilding kit. Use a small pad of folded cheesecloth to press the leaf onto the surface. The pad will prevent the oils in your skin from discoloring the leaf and any fingerprints being left on the surface. Make sure the cheesecloth does not touch the size. [photo E]

7 BEFORE REMOVING THE PAINTER'S TAPE, SCORE AROUND the edges of each of the gilded squares with a new single-edge razor blade, cutting all the way through the metal leaf and size to the surface of the table. Make sure to cut all the way through so as not to disturb the leaf that has been applied to the squares as you remove the tape. [photo F]

8 CAREFULLY REMOVE THE TAPE FROM THE TABLE. APPLY 1 OR 2 coats of the acrylic varnish to seal the surface of the gilded squares only, if desired. Place the glass on the tabletop to protect the surface.

Folding Card Table

MY FATHER HAD THIS TABLE IN HIS BASEMENT FOR MANY YEARS AND WAS ABOUT TO CONSIGN IT TO THE TRASH ONE DAY WHEN I HAPPENED TO BE VISITING. I WAS IMMEDIATELY DRAWN TO THE FLORAL IMAGE ON THE TOP AND SO TOOK IT HOME WITH THE INTENTION OF TAKING THE CARDBOARD TOP OFF AND FRAMING IT. IT SAT AROUND FOR A LONG TIME BEFORE I LOOKED AT IT AGAIN. AND WHEN I DID, I HAPPENED TO NEED AN EXTRA TABLE FOR A SPECIAL OCCASION. I DECIDED THAT IT WAS REALLY A VERY USEFUL AND SWEET LITTLE TABLE TO HAVE. IT FOLDS OUT OF THE WAY WHEN YOU DON'T NEED IT AND CAN BE USED IN ANY NUMBER OF WAYS AND FOR A MULTITUDE OF TASKS SUCH AS IMPROMPTU DINING INDOORS OR OUT, AN EXTRA WORK SURFACE, AND EVEN FOR ITS ORIGINAL USE AS A CARD TABLE.

materials

- Folding table
- Wood saw
- 1/8-inch medium-density fiberboard
- Wood glue
- Wood dowel
- Sandpaper
- Small paintbrush
- Water-based wood stain
- Cheesecloth or clean rag
- Ruler
- Scissors
- Artist's linen
- Iron
- Fusible web
- Soft lead pencil
- Masking tape in two widths: 1/4-inch and 1 1/2-inch
- Concentrated artist's acrylic in complementary colors
- Small dish
- Stenciling brush
- Small finishing nails

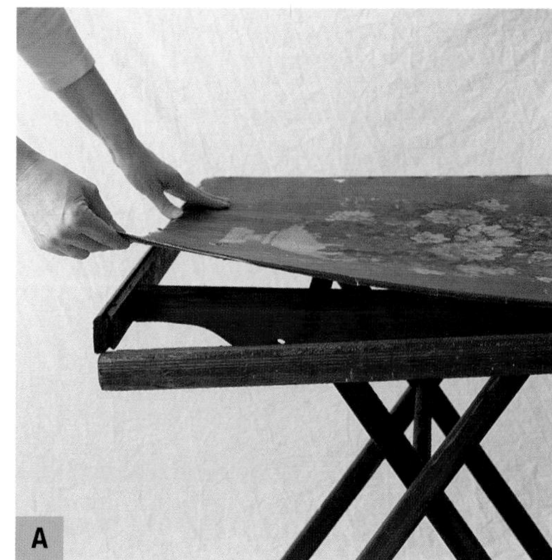

A

1 REMOVE THE ORIGINAL CARDBOARD TABLETOP FROM THE table frame and use it as a pattern to cut a new top out of 1/8-inch fiberboard. Set both aside. [photo A]

2 INSPECT THE TABLE FRAME AND LEGS FOR ANY MISSING pieces (mine was missing a dowel) or loose joints. Remove any loose nails and reglue the corners using wood glue. Apply glue liberally to the joint and press the 2 sides together. Wipe excess glue away from the joint with a clean cloth. Renail the corners of the frame together if necessary. Let the glue dry completely. I also cut a length of dowel to replace the missing piece and glued it in place.

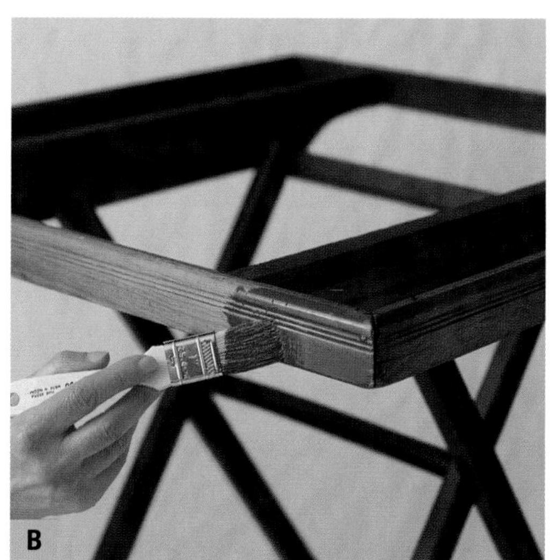

B

3 IF NEEDED, USE A WOOD REFINISHING PRODUCT OR PAINT stripper to remove the old finish. Here a light sanding was enough to remove the little bit of finish that was left on the wood.

4 WITH THE SMALL PAINTBRUSH, LIBERALLY APPLY THE water-based stain, working on a small area at a time, following the directions on the container. Allow the stain to penetrate the surface no longer than 3 to 5 minutes. [photo B]

5 WHILE THE STAIN IS STILL WET, USE A PIECE OF CHEESE-cloth or clean soft rag to wipe off the excess, working in the direction of the wood grain. Continue until frame is completely stained. Set frame aside. [photo C]

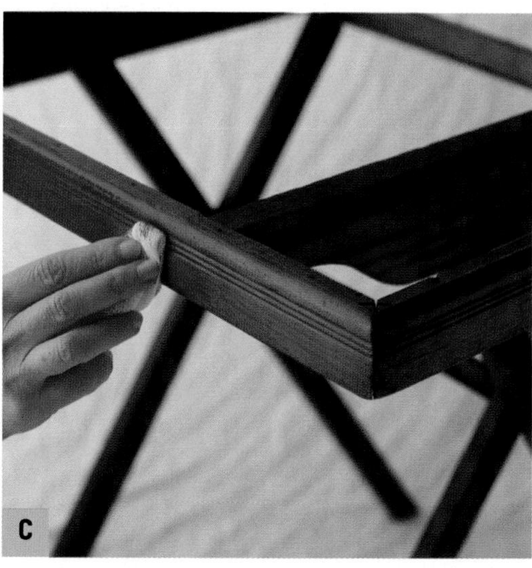

C

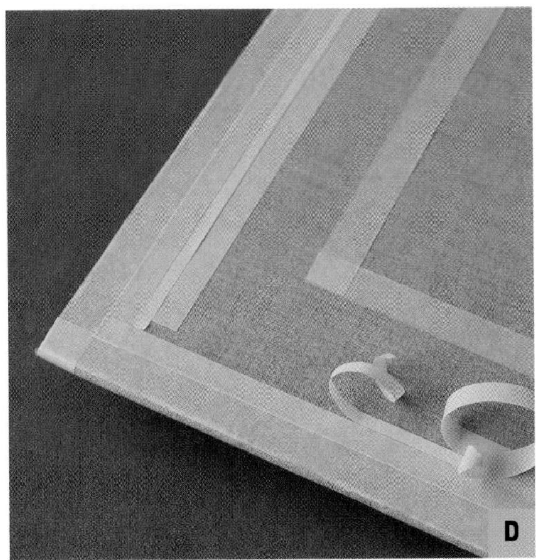
D

6 MAKE THE NEW FABRIC-COVERED TOP AS FOLLOWS: MEASURE the fiberboard top and cut a piece of artist's linen to those dimensions, adding 2 inches to each side for turning. Iron the fusible web to the wrong side of the fabric, following the manufacturer's directions. Center the fabric, right-side up and fusible-side down, on the fiberboard top. Trim the excess fabric by cutting triangles of the linen ½ inch away from the fiberboard corners. Again following directions, use the iron to fuse the fabric to the board. Turn over and wrap the excess fabric to the back of the board; fuse in place as before.

7 DECIDE ON THE WIDTH OF THE 2 STRIPES TO BE PAINTED on the tabletop. Here the narrow stripe is ¼ inch wide and the wide stripe is 1½ inches wide. Either draw directly on the canvas with a pencil to mark the lines for the stripes or use the width of the masking tape itself as a measure.

E

8 MEASURE THE BORDER AREA THAT WILL REMAIN unpainted and mask it off with 1 or 2 rows of masking tape. Mark the space for the narrow stripe by laying down a line of the ¼-inch masking tape around the perimeter of the previously masked-off border. This narrow band of masking tape can then be removed when you are ready to paint the narrower stripe. Mask off the areas on either side of the wider stripe that will not be painted with strips of the masking tape to protect them while you are painting the 1½-inch stripe. [photo D]

9 POUR A SMALL AMOUNT OF THE FIRST COLOR OF PAINT INTO a dish. Using the stencil brush, daub the paint onto the canvas, completely covering the wider stripe with the paint. When the paint is dry, remove the ¼-inch-wide masking tape to expose the unpainted canvas for the narrower stripe. Pour a small amount of the second color of paint in a dish. Carefully daub the second paint onto the canvas, completely covering the narrow stripe. When the paint is completely dry, remove all the remaining masking tape. [photos E and F]

F

10 PLACE THE FINISHED TOP ON THE BASE AND ATTACH WITH small finishing nails.

End Table with Drawer

THERE'S NOT A LOT OF DETAIL ON THIS SMALL END TABLE, AND IT'S NOT PARTICULARLY WELL MADE, SO THIS IS EXACTLY THE KIND OF PIECE THAT IS TOO EASILY OVERLOOKED AT A HOUSE SALE OR FLEA MARKET. WHEN I BOUGHT THIS TABLE, IT WASN'T PAINTED WHITE SO IT WAS EVEN MORE UNNOTICEABLE. HOWEVER, I LIKED THE SQUARE, VAGUELY MISSION-INSPIRED LEGS, THE RECESSED SHAPE FOR THE DRAWER PULL, AND OF COURSE, THE AFFORDABLE PRICE. WITH A SIMPLE PIECE LIKE THIS, A COAT OF PAINT IN AN UNEXPECTED COLOR LIKE PURPLE TRANSFORMS IT INTO A MUCH MORE INTERESTING OBJECT. ULTIMATELY, THE UNUSUAL SHADE LENDS THE TABLE A DISTINCTIVE AIR—A GOOD TRICK TO REMEMBER WHENEVER YOU FIND THIS KIND OF NONDESCRIPT PIECE.

materials

End table	Wood putty
Wood glue	Putty knife
Hammer	Sandpaper
Clamp	Household paintbrush
Wood block	Satin finish water-based paint

1 INSPECT THE TABLE AND DRAWER FOR LOOSE JOINTS. Remove any loose nails and reglue any loose joints in the drawer using wood glue. Apply the glue liberally to the joint and press the 2 sides together. Wipe any excess glue away from the joint with a clean cloth. Renail the joints on the drawer together, if necessary. Clamp or place weights on the joint until the glue sets and is completely dry. [photos A and B]

2 OPEN THE JOINT ON THE LEG AS WIDE AS POSSIBLE. APPLY glue to the legs using the nozzle on the bottle to direct the glue inside the opening. Tap the joints together lightly using a hammer and a wood block to protect the surface. Let the glue dry before proceeding. [photo C]

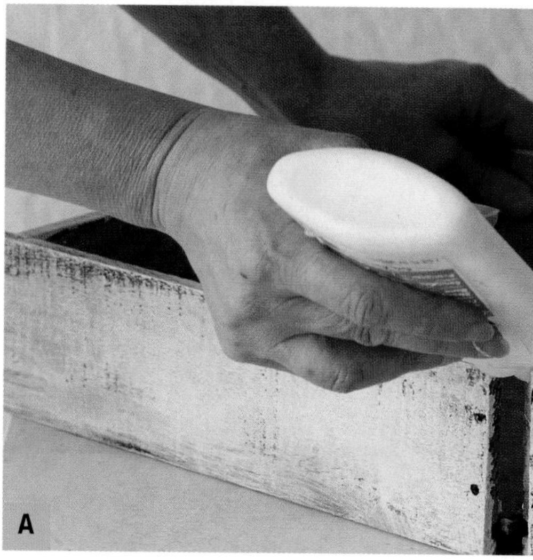

A

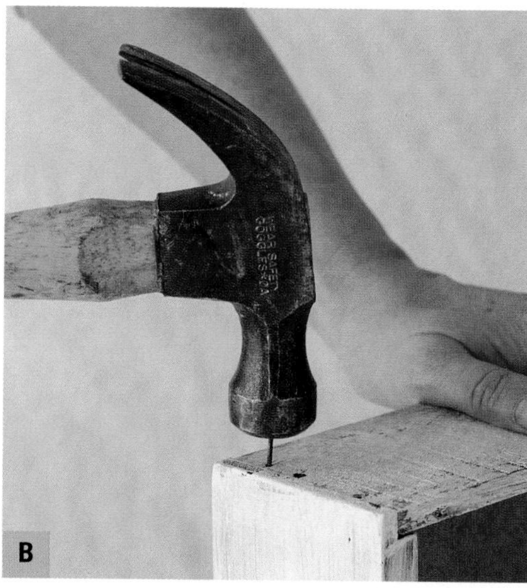

B

C

loose drawer pulls

Many old drawers pull open with wooden knobs that fasten from the inside with a screw. Frequently these screws loosen over time because the threads inside the wooden knob are stripped. To fix, dip a piece of string in wood glue and wind it around the threads of the screw, working it into the grooves. Insert the screw through the drawer and screw the knob back on. Let the glue dry before using.

D

E

F

3 APPLY WOOD PUTTY OVER ANY CHIPS, CRACKS, OR OTHER blemishes on the surface. Deeper holes might need more than one application of putty. Push the putty down into the cracks with the putty knife. Draw the knife across the surface, smoothing the excess putty as you go. [photo D]

4 LET THE PUTTY DRY UNTIL IT IS HARD. SAND THE SURFACE lightly with fine-grade sandpaper. Prime the piece if necessary. [photo E]

5 PAINT WITH 2 COATS OF SATIN FINISH WATER-BASED PAINT. Let dry completely between coats and after the final coat. [photo F]

storing and organizing

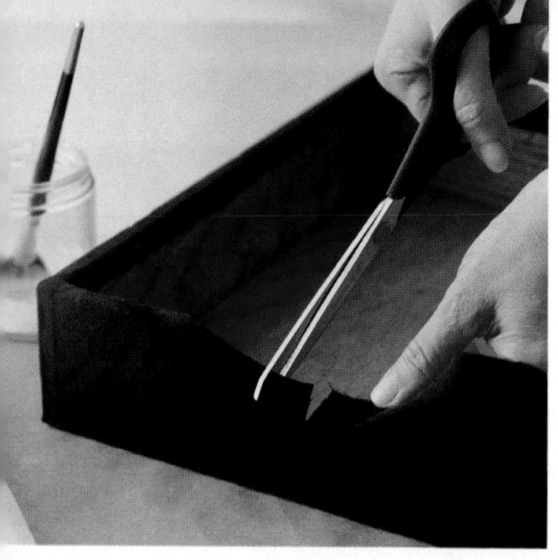

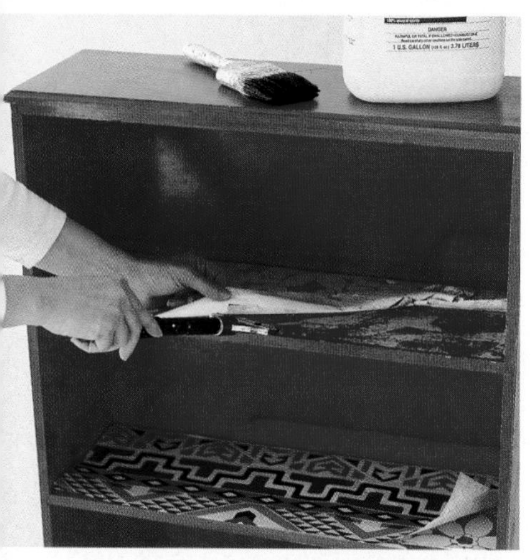

we all know that you can

never have too much storage space, but what you may not realize is that creating order in your home can be a stylish process as well. In my family, everyone has about twenty different hobbies and interests, and it's a creative challenge to keep our home from feeling disordered and cluttered. Having everything you need in one place—like writing paper and pens on your desk—eliminates unnecessary stress by streamlining the functions of a space. If you start by assessing where and what kind of storage each room needs, you can look for reasonably priced pieces that will bring a sense of order to that ever expanding clutter. Old pieces can be turned to new uses—like a metal vegetable bin used to store towels—and decorated to fit in with the space so that they become attractive additions as well. Use your imagination to create storage opportunities.

For many years, even after our son, Alex, was born, my husband and I lived in a tiny apartment. We were forced to be relentlessly creative about storage—everything was scrutinized for its usefulness and anything extraneous banished (this was long before my days of rescuing other people's castoffs). Everything in that apartment had its place just like the living quarters of a ship. Now our constant challenge is to contain all of our interests and collections with the added space of a house. We always seem to be in need of more bookshelves for housing all our books and a growing number of CDs, for displaying collections of glass and pottery, for keeping art and craft supplies accessible.

Bookcases really are the most versatile kind of storage space. I have at least one in almost every room of my house that I use for a range of purposes, from storing games in my son's room to showcasing a collection of pottery in the dining room, or as my friend Annette does, for storing a stellar collection of vintage tablecloths and linens in her dining area. Bookcases like these can also have multiple uses over their lifetime, moving from one room to another as your needs and situation change.

Consequently I'm always on the lookout for small and medium-sized wooden bookcases. They do turn up, though less often than some of the other pieces in this book. If you find one, buy it—even if you don't know where you might use it at that moment. A bookcase like this can be easily painted and dressed up with moldings to give it more character. Metal shelving too can be rehabilitated; look where used office furniture is sold.

Anything with hooks is also great. Being inherently lazy, I love tossing a coat, scarf, or hat over a hook by the door. Coatracks or other old wall-mounted racks with hooks or pegs are extremely useful and practical. If you can't find a wooden one, look for the older and more common utilitarian metal ones that have their own rough charm. Single metal hooks can be cleaned up and mounted on a piece of painted board to hang near a door. And don't forget that there's something deliciously and doubly satisfying about adding pieces to your home that are as practical as they are pretty.

Dear Vince,
Thanks for all
your help and

Wooden Letter Box

OLD WOODEN BOXES LIKE THIS ARE FAIRLY PLENTIFUL AT FLEA MARKETS, BUT PRACTICALLY ANY TYPE OF BOX OR CONTAINER CAN BE COVERED WITH FABRIC. THIS TECHNIQUE IS ESPECIALLY SUITED TO BOXES WITH SCARRED AND SCRATCHED SURFACES WITHOUT ANY PATINA WORTH PRESERVING, SO WHEN YOU NEXT FALL IN LOVE WITH THE SHAPE, SIZE, OR PRICE OF A BEAT-UP BOX, REMEMBER THIS OPTION.

THE FABRIC I USED FOR THIS BOX CAME FROM A FAVORITE PAIR OF SILK TWILL PANTS THAT I COULDN'T BEAR TO DISCARD EVEN THOUGH THEY WERE NO LONGER WEARABLE. THE SUEDE PAPER LINING WAS AN ART STORE DISCOVERY THAT LOOKS JUST LIKE THE REAL THING BUT IS MUCH SIMPLER TO WORK WITH AND, OF COURSE, LESS EXPENSIVE. IT ALSO CONTRASTS BEAUTIFULLY WITH THE TEXTURE OF THE MATTE SILK FABRIC. ONCE I'VE HIT UPON A GOOD THING, I LIKE TO EXPAND ON IT AND THIS PROJECT IS PARTICULARLY SUITED TO MULTIPLES. YOU COULD COVER THREE OR FOUR DIFFERENT BOXES IN MATCHING OR COORDINATING FABRICS AND STACK THEM ON A DESK. AND IF YOU CAN'T FIND WOODEN BOXES, STIFF CARDBOARD ONES WORK JUST AS WELL AND ARE JUST AS EASY TO COVER.

materials

- Wooden letter box
- Silk twill fabric or other sturdy fabric
- Light color tailor's chalk or fabric marking pen
- Ruler
- Scissors
- Tracing paper
- Soft lead pencil
- Fan-shaped artist's brush
- Small dish or jar for glue
- Craft glue
- Suede paper or other lining material
- White pencil

1 MEASURE THE BOTTOM OF THE BOX AND TO each dimension add twice the depth of the sides of the box, plus a total of $1\frac{1}{2}$ inches for turning. Cut a piece of the fabric to those dimensions. Center the box, faceup, on the wrong side of the fabric. Mark the position of the bottom of the box with the tailor's chalk.

2 MARK A POINT MEASURING $\frac{1}{4}$ INCH DIAGonally outward from each corner. Cut out a square of fabric at each corner, following the lines of the marked point. Snip to the corner of the box. Fold under the narrow edge at each corner and press.

3 USING THE TRACING PAPER AND THE LEAD pencil, trace the shape of the curve on the front of the box. Cut out a pattern from the tracing paper. Place the paper on the front edge of the fabric, trace its contour, and cut the shape out. [all the above—photo A]

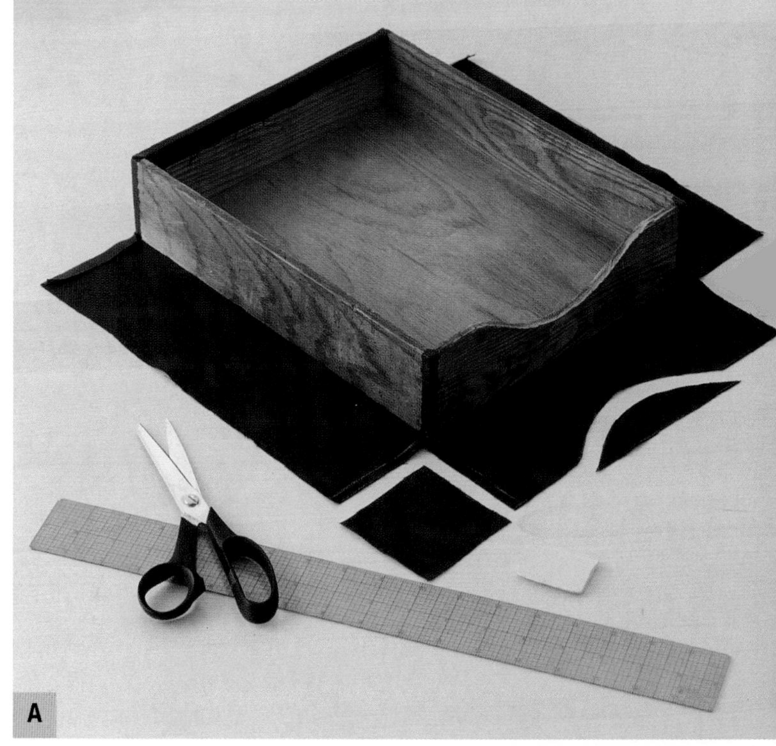

A

4 WITH THE BRUSH, COVER THE BOTTOM OF THE BOX WITH THE glue and position the box on top of the fabric. Glue the box in place, smoothing the fabric. Turn up the back piece of the fabric and glue in place, then turn the overhang to the inside and glue in place. Trim the fabric at the inside corners if necessary before folding in and gluing to the inside of the box. Turn up the side pieces of the fabric and glue in place as above. [photo B]

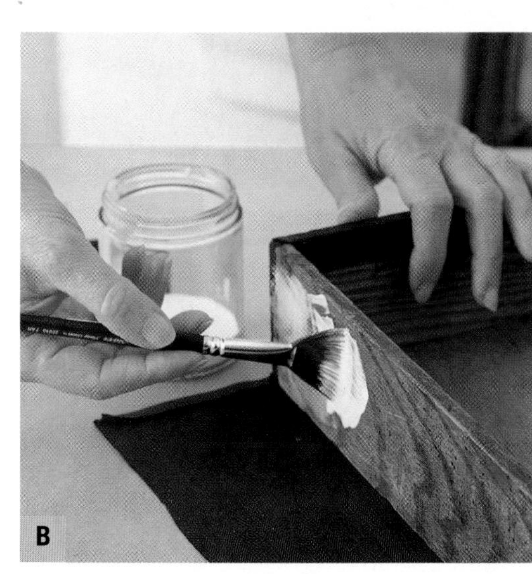

B

5 BEFORE TURNING THE FABRIC ON THE FRONT CURVED SECtion to the inside, carefully clip along the inside edge in several

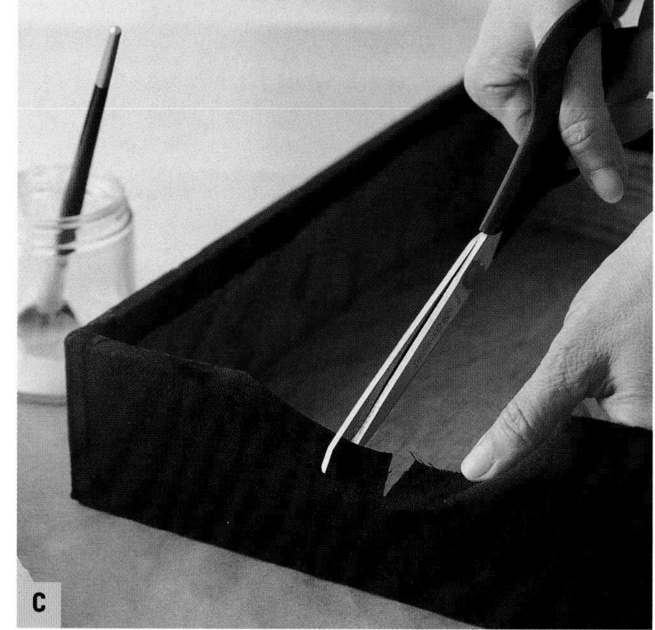
C

places so it will lie flat and then glue the fabric to the inside of the box. [photo C]

6 TO LINE THE BOX, MEASURE THE INSIDE BOTTOM and to each dimension add twice the depth of the sides of the box. Cut the lining material to those dimensions. Mark the inside dimensions of the box on the wrong side of the lining with the white pencil, extending the lines out to the edges of the paper. Cut a square out of each corner, following the marked lines. Cut the shaped front curve out, using the pattern made in step 3. [photo D]

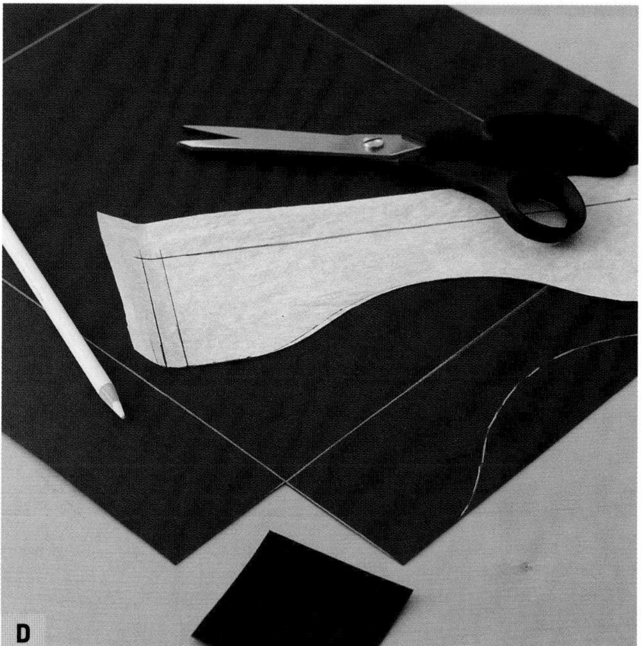
D

7 PLACE THE PAPER ON A HARD SURFACE, RIGHT-SIDE up. Crease and fold the paper along the marked lines on each side. [photo E]

8 TEST THE LINING TO MAKE SURE IT FITS INSIDE THE box. Make any adjustments needed and glue in place. [photo F]

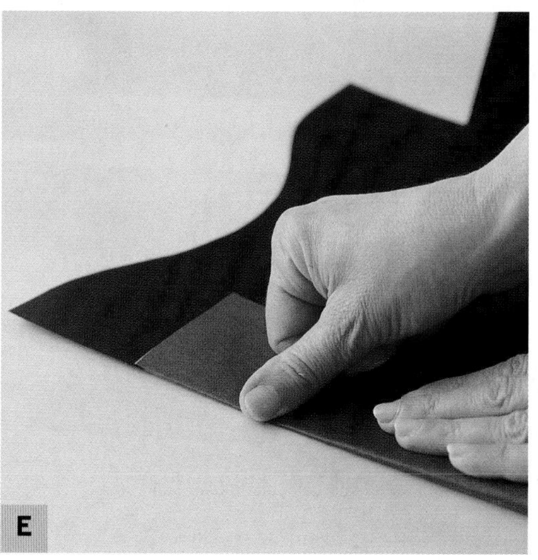
E

F

Narrow Bookcase

WHEN I BROUGHT THIS SMALL BOOKCASE HOME FROM THE SALVATION ARMY STORE, IT WAS COVERED IN BRIGHT ORANGE PAINT AND HAD TWO LAYERS OF ADHESIVE PAPER ON THE SHELVES. I LIKED ITS SIMPLE SHAPE, AND ASIDE FROM THE PAINT, IT WAS IN VERY GOOD CONDITION AND COST ONLY $35. WITH THE ADDITION OF SOME INEXPENSIVE STOCK MOLDING, I KNEW IT COULD BE A KNOCKOUT. SOMETIMES THE PRICE OF A PLAIN BUT STURDY BOOKCASE IS TOO ENTICING TO PASS UP, BUT THIS DOESN'T MEAN YOU HAVE TO SETTLE FOR ITS STARK LINES.

materials

Bookcase	Wood saw
Paint thinner	Darker shade satin finish water-based paint
Household paintbrush	Lighter shade satin finish water-based paint
Wallpaper scraper	Foam roller/tray
Power sander	Acrylic primer
Corner blocks	Wood glue
Molding (assorted widths, styles)	Masking tape
Tape measure	Clamps
Soft lead pencil	

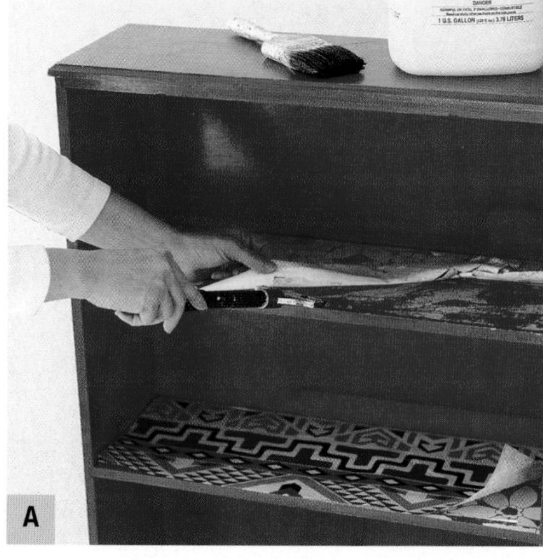
A

1 IF THE SHELVES ARE LINED WITH CONTACT PAPER, REMOVE it by using the paint thinner to loosen the adhesive. Apply the thinner with a brush under the paper and use a wallpaper scraper to remove the loosened paper from the shelves. [photo A]

2 SAND THE BOOKCASE AS MUCH AS NECESSARY TO REMOVE the gloss from the existing paint.

B

3 CUT THE DIFFERENT MOLDINGS IN THIS SEQUENCE: FIRST, lay the corner blocks on the top outside corners, then measure the length of each side below the blocks. Mark the pilaster molding and cut 2 pieces to fit each of the side lengths just measured. Next measure across the width of the bookcase along the front edge of each shelf. Cut out pieces to correspond with each measurement for the front edge of each shelf and the front edges of the top and the bottom shelves. With the pencil, indicate on the back where each piece goes for easy assembly later. [photo B]

4 PAINT THE INSIDE OF THE BOOKCASE WITH 2 COATS OF THE darker paint. Paint the outside of the bookcase with 2 coats of the lighter paint. Prime all the trims, including the molding for the top piece, with the acrylic primer and when the primer is dry, paint with 2 coats of the lighter paint. Let the paint dry thoroughly between coats and after the last coat. [photo C]

C

5 LAY THE BOOKCASE ON ITS BACK AND GLUE THE TRIMS AND the molding in place along the sides, shelves, and top and bottom edges with the wood glue. Use masking tape to hold the trim in place as the glue dries if necessary. After the glue is dry, carefully remove the tape and stand the bookcase up. [photo D]

D

6 TO MAKE THE FRAME THAT SITS ON top of the bookcase, measure across the sides and front edge of the bookcase top. Cut 3 pieces out of beaded trim to those measurements, mitering the 2 front corners. Glue the pieces together at each corner with the wood glue and then glue the frame to the top of the bookcase, resting it on the front top edge. Clamp until the glue is dry. [photo E]

E

using moldings

You can find decorative moldings like those I've used here at any lumberyard or, for a better selection, try a specialty building material store. The choices are numerous, from the pilaster moldings and corner blocks used on the long sides to the decorative beaded molding used on the top. Paint the moldings slightly lighter or darker than the bookcase itself for a contrasting accent. You can do this with any type of older bookcase or even with a new one. And if you have two different bookcases that you want to place in the same room, complementary moldings and paint color will give the illusion that they're a matching pair despite slight differences in their respective sizes.

Mission-Style Coatrack

THE SIMPLE MISSION-INSPIRED SHAPE OF THIS COATRACK HAD A STURDY, UTILITARIAN APPEAL, BUT THE LEGS WERE WOBBLY, THE HOOKS PITTED AND PAINT-COVERED, AND THE COLOR OFF-PUTTING. I WANTED TO EMPHASIZE THE CURVE OF THE BENT WOODEN LEGS AND THE NEATLY TURNED FINIAL ON TOP AND SO I DECIDED TO PAINT THEM A DARKER SHADE OF THE PAINT COLOR I CHOSE FOR THE UPRIGHT PIECE. THE TWO SHADES OF YELLOW WORK NICELY TOGETHER: THE EGG YOLK IS JUST DIFFERENT ENOUGH TO SHOW OFF THE SMOOTH, BOLD SHAPE OF THE LEGS AND THE DETAILS ON THE FINIAL, BUT NOT TOO JARRING AGAINST THE LIGHTER YELLOW. THIS CONTRASTING COMBINATION WORKS FOR A VARIETY OF COLORS, SO FEEL FREE TO EXPERIMENT WITH GREENS, BLUES, OR SHADES OF WHITE.

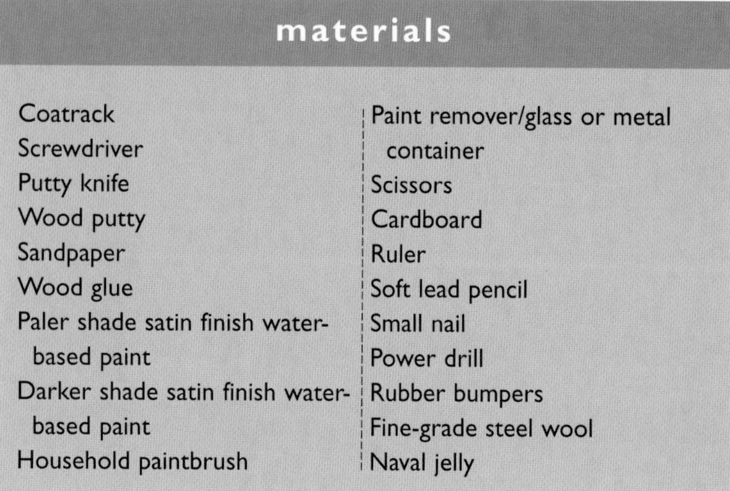

materials

Coatrack	Paint remover/glass or metal container
Screwdriver	Scissors
Putty knife	Cardboard
Wood putty	Ruler
Sandpaper	Soft lead pencil
Wood glue	Small nail
Paler shade satin finish water-based paint	Power drill
Darker shade satin finish water-based paint	Rubber bumpers
Household paintbrush	Fine-grade steel wool
	Naval jelly

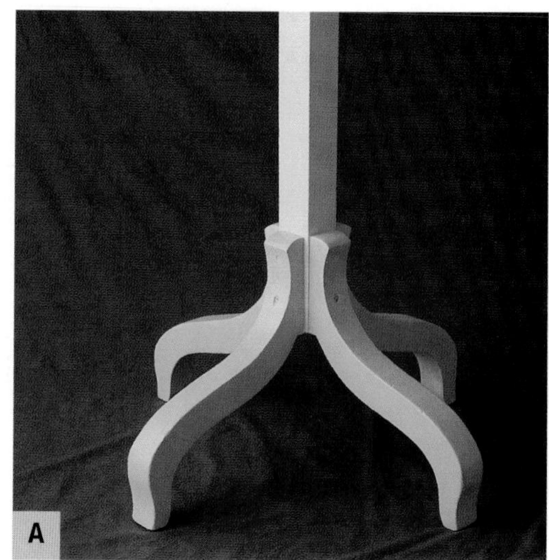

A

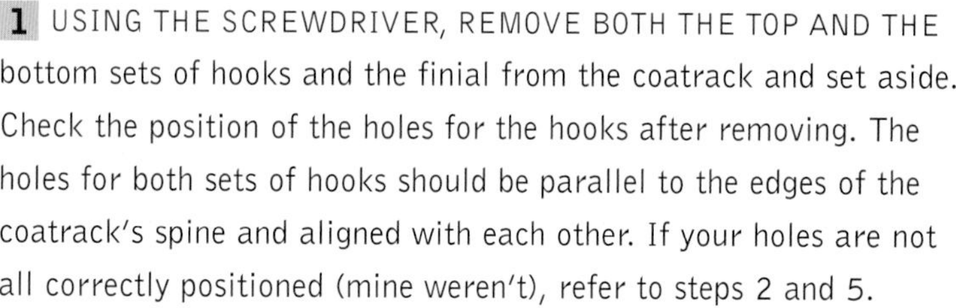

1 USING THE SCREWDRIVER, REMOVE BOTH THE TOP AND THE bottom sets of hooks and the finial from the coatrack and set aside. Check the position of the holes for the hooks after removing. The holes for both sets of hooks should be parallel to the edges of the coatrack's spine and aligned with each other. If your holes are not all correctly positioned (mine weren't), refer to steps 2 and 5.

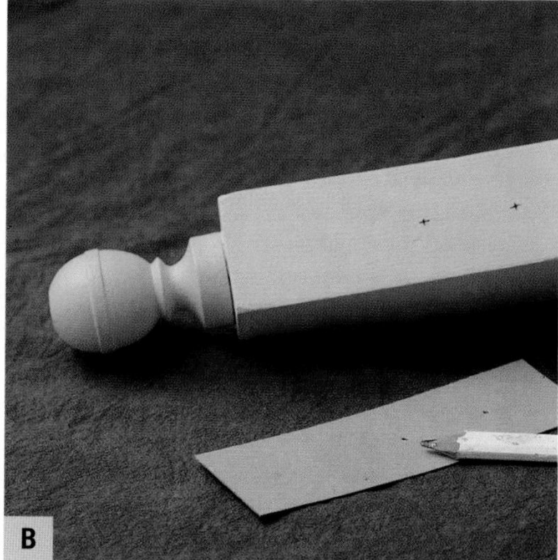

B

2 USING A PUTTY KNIFE, FILL ANY OF THE HOLES THAT MIGHT need repositioning with wood putty. When the putty is dry, sand to a smooth finish. Glue any loose joints on the legs if necessary, using the wood glue. Let the glue dry completely.

3 SAND THE COATRACK AS NEEDED TO REMOVE THE OLD PAINT. Paint the whole piece, including the legs, with the pale color paint. Paint the finial as well. After the first coat is dry, sand if necessary, then apply a second coat of the pale color to the upright piece only.

4 WHEN DRY, PAINT THE LEGS AND FINIAL WITH 2 COATS OF the darker satin finish water-based paint, letting each coat dry thoroughly. When dry, reattach the finial to the coatrack. [photo A]

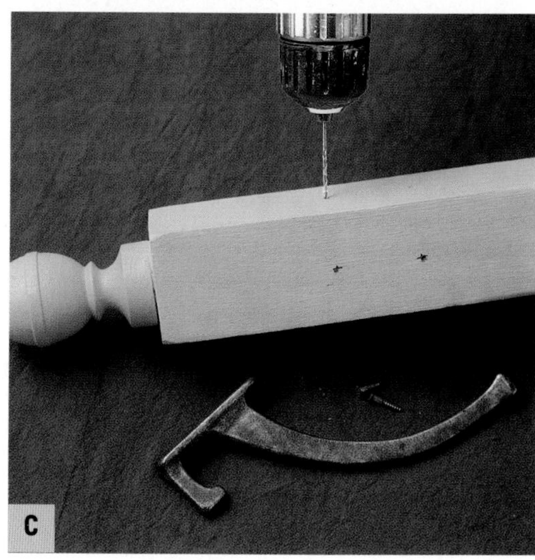

C

D

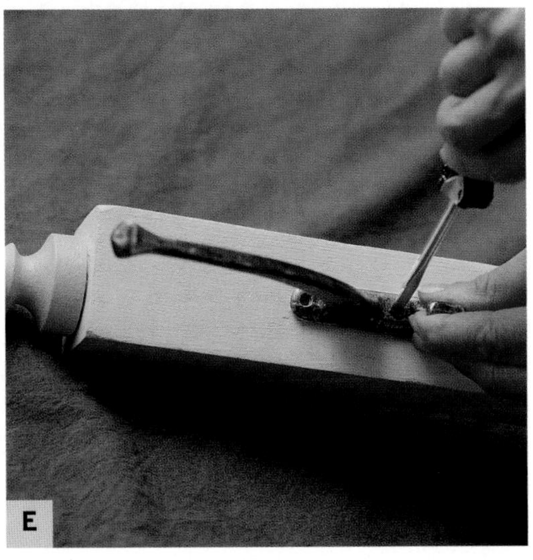
E

to remove rust

If the hooks are a little rusty, you can easily clean them. After removing the paint from the hooks, use a fine grade of steel wool dipped in naval jelly or vegetable oil to remove any rust from the surface. Light rust can also be removed by scrubbing with turpentine. Make sure to wear protective gloves when working with solvents such as naval jelly or turpentine. If necessary, the hooks can be further cleaned and polished using a buffing pad on a power drill.

F

5 MAKE A TEMPLATE TO MARK THE POSITION OF THE NEW holes for the hooks by cutting a small piece of cardboard to the same width as the side of the upright where the hook will go. Align the top edge of the cardboard piece with the top edge of the coatrack. Place a hook on the cardboard, lining it up so that the new holes fall in the desired positions. Mark the position of the holes on the cardboard with a pencil. Use a small nail to make holes in the cardboard where marked. [photo B]

6 USING THE TEMPLATE AND A PENCIL, MARK THE NEW HOLES for the top hooks on all 4 sides of the coatrack. Drill starter holes for the screws. [photo C]

7 IF THE HARDWARE HAS BEEN PAINTED, SOAK IT IN THE PAINT remover to remove any old paint. Scrape or wipe off the paint when it softens. [photo D]

8 REATTACH THE TOP HOOKS WITH SCREWS, USING THE NEW holes on all 4 sides of the coatrack. Reattach the bottom hooks with screws, using the existing holes. [photo E]

9 ATTACH THE RUBBER BUMPERS TO THE BOTTOM OF EACH LEG with the screws. [photo F]

Metal Storage Bin

STANDING BINS OF THIS TYPE WERE ORIGINALLY USED IN KITCHENS AND PANTRIES TO STORE ROOT VEGETABLES SUCH AS ONIONS AND POTATOES. I LOVE THE STAMPED AND PIERCED METAL—IT HAS A MODERN, ALMOST INDUSTRIAL FEEL—AND IT'S VERY FUNCTIONAL AS WELL, WITH ITS DEEP BOTTOM SHELF, SLANTED MIDDLE SHELF FOR EASY ACCESS, AND THE DIVIDED STORAGE AREA ON TOP. BY ADDING A GLASS TOP, I MADE IT EVEN MORE USEFUL WITHOUT DISTRACTING FROM THE CLEAN SHAPE AND SLEEK MATERIALS. SO WHILE ITS ORIGINAL FUNCTION HAS CHANGED, IT STILL OFFERS THE SAME GREAT STORAGE SPACE IN ITS NEW SETTING. ANY MIRROR OR GLASS STORE CAN CUT A PIECE OF GLASS TO SIZE FOR THE TOP. THE TEXTURED GLASS TOP (LIKE THOSE FOUND ON METAL OUTDOOR FURNITURE) ADDS A PLEASING AND EASY-TO-CLEAN SURFACE. GLUE RUBBER BUMPERS TO THE UNDERSIDE OF THE GLASS TO KEEP IT STEADY AND IN PLACE ON TOP OF THE BIN.

materials

- Metal bin
- Wire brush
- Steel wool
- Spray paint (I used Rust-oleum's "Hammered Metal Finish" in silver)
- ¼-inch-thick textured glass
- Wax crayon
- Rubber bumpers
- Clear silicone glue

1 USING A WIRE BRUSH, REMOVE ANY LOOSE PAINT ON THE bin. Clean any rusty areas with steel wool. Working in a well-ventilated area, spray the bin with 2 coats of paint. Let it dry completely between each coat and after the last coat. [photo A]

2 MEASURE THE TOP OF THE BIN AND ADD 4 INCHES TO EACH dimension. Have a piece of ¼-inch-thick glass cut to that size for a top. Make sure to have the edges polished and the corners slightly rounded.

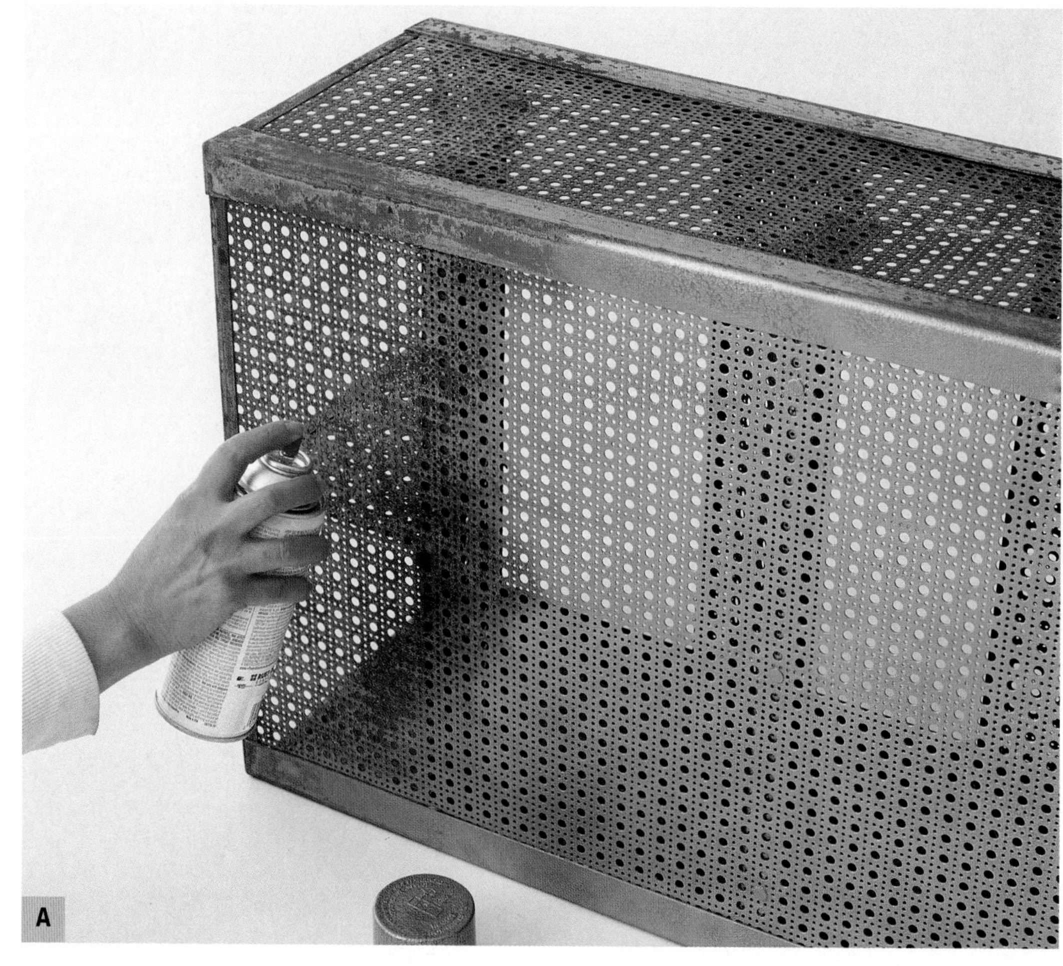

A

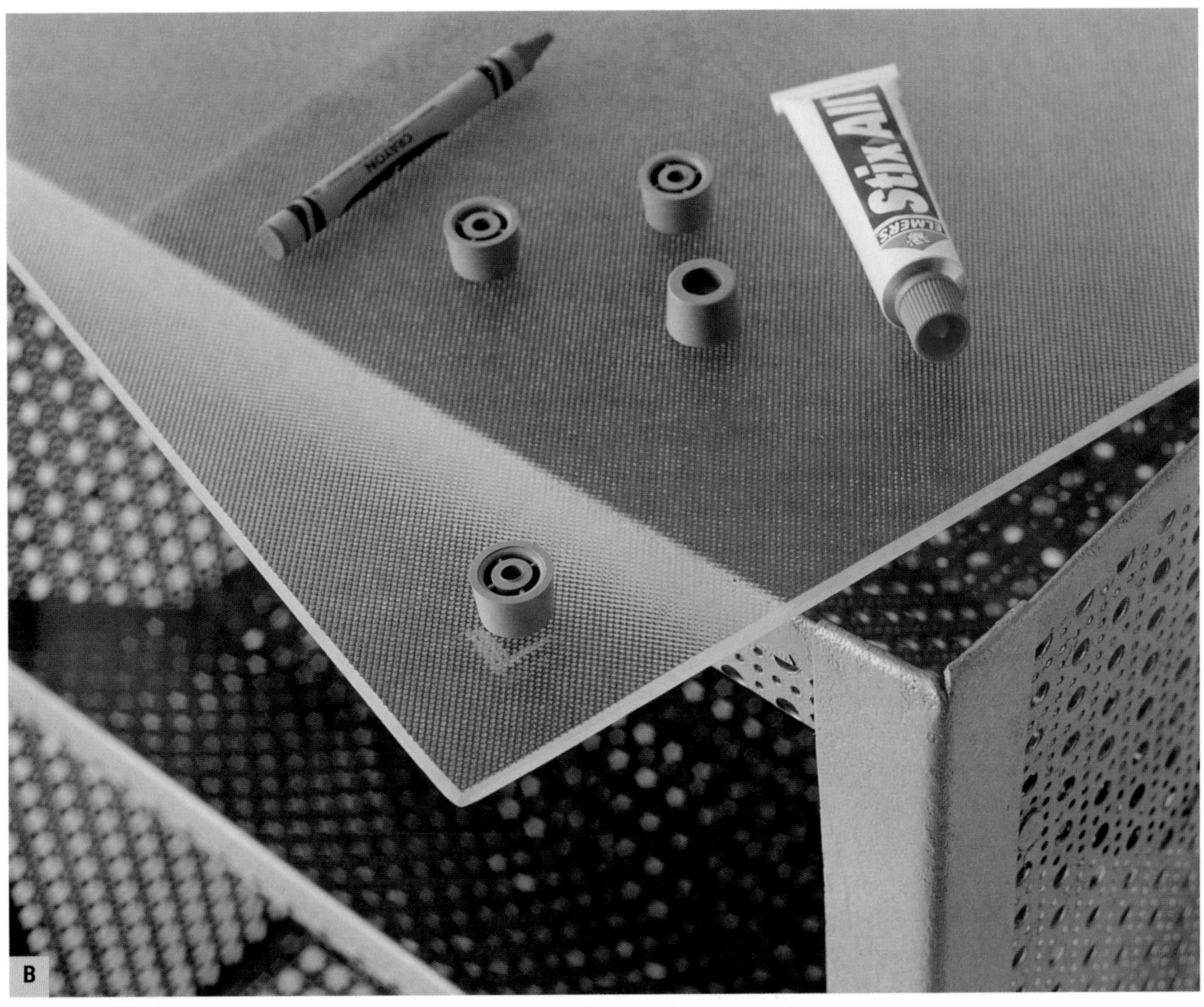

B

choosing the glass tabletop

Instead of using a piece of plain glass for a tabletop, ask your local glazier to show you samples of the different surface textures and colors they have on hand or can order for you. Some of the available options include rippled, hammered, fluted, cross-hatched, or opaque or tinted glass. As I did here, you can opt for the visual drama that a piece of textured or colored glass will bring to your piece. A thickness of ¼ inch to ½ inch is best for tabletops.

3 CENTER THE GLASS ON THE BIN, RIGHT-SIDE UP, AND USE the crayon to make a mark just to the inside of all 4 corners lightly on the surface of the glass. Turn the glass over and following the corner marks, glue a rubber bumper in each corner just to the inside of each corner mark, using the clear silicone glue. Let it dry completely. [photo B]

4 TURN THE GLASS FACEUP AND PLACE ON THE BIN SO THE bumpers are positioned just inside of each corner. Remove the crayon marks left on the topside by rubbing lightly with a paper towel.

odds and ends

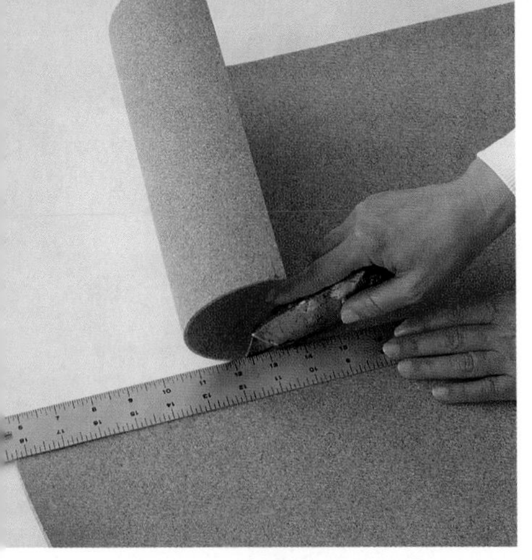

stuffed under the tables at flea markets or half hidden in thrift shops, old tatty cardboard boxes can yield some of the most interesting candidates for makeovers. That's where the smaller items, like picture frames, can be found, and they have the advantage of being easy to transport, so they can be bought on impulse. Frames can quickly lift a room and I think my walls would feel quite naked without them. Fortunately it's the rare flea market, garage sale, or thrift store that doesn't yield a bumper crop of interesting old frames. I like to keep a cache on hand, from small oval portrait frames to larger rectangular ones and everything in between, to give as gifts—perhaps filled with a print, photo, or even a clipping. Try not to get distracted by the pictures or art in the frames—though sometimes you can find neat images—it's the frames and not what's in them that you're buying. When possible, choose wooden frames rather than plastic and make sure the molding is in good shape. If it is loose, any frame can be reattached at the corners and then repainted or even stripped. The glass can be easily replaced if it is scratched or dull and should never factor into your decision.

Old trays are other frequent finds, and they are extremely useful. Refurbished trays are an ideal way to house even more flea market finds such as a collection of glass bottles, small jewelry boxes, or paperweights. Also, an odd collection of trays repainted in the same color can serve at the dining table as place mats for a more unusual setting. Look for unique shapes and a variety of sizes; a wide range will make them more practical for diverse uses. When used to serve food, an attractive tray can bring a polished look even to a take-out meal or can complete a luxurious breakfast in bed. I also like the way haphazard things take on the appearance of a collection when unified by a tray. There are dozens of possibilities: on a dresser or nightstand to hold reading glasses, water glasses, and other small objects; in the bathroom to organize bottles and makeup; or on a small table to organize a bar area with bottles, decanters, as well as a few glasses.

Metal trays are very inexpensive, easy to find, and can be decorated in a variety of ways. The simplest way to pick them up is to spray paint them with either a glossy paint or one of the newer metallic spray paints. If you are more ambitious, you could create a pretty decoupage on the surface. No matter what you decide to do with your trays, a small stock of them will always come in handy.

Folding screens represent some of my all-time favorite finds because they are both extremely handsome and practical. I like to think of them as instant and flexible architectural devices, whether you're looking to create divisions within one large room or mask some unsightly equipment. For the pack rats among us, screens are especially good for hiding a stash that's gotten out of control. I like to keep one next to my desk to hide the mess that frequently accumulates there. If you cover one side with cork, you've essentially added a large bulletin board adjacent to the desk. Screens can also fit easily in any room and I love the way they can bring instant tranquility to any space by blocking off a distracting area of chaos.

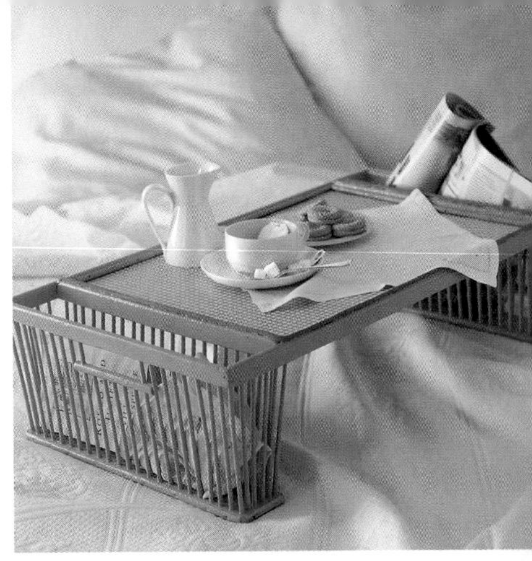

Picture Frames

SOMETIMES THE BEST WORN TREASURES COME FROM FRIENDS, AND THESE OVAL FRAMED RED ROSE PRINTS THAT HAIL FROM MY FRIENDS CHARLIE AND ARTEMIS ARE PRIME EXAMPLES. THE FRAMES NEEDED SOME ATTENTION, BUT THE FADED FLORAL IMAGES HAD A NOSTALGIC APPEAL. THE PRINTS AREN'T FANCY BOTANICALS, BUT I FIND THEM EXTREMELY CHARMING. THE RED ROSES BRIGHTEN AGAINST THE MAT'S TURQUOISE LINE. IT'S FAIRLY EASY TO FIND SIMILAR TYPES OF FLORAL IMAGES ALREADY FRAMED OR TO MAKE YOUR OWN, AS I DID HERE SO THAT THE RED FRAMES MATCHED THE OVAL FRAMED ROSES. JUST MAKE A PHOTOCOPY OF YOUR CHOSEN FLOWER IMAGE ON A COLOR COPIER, ADJUSTING THE SIZE TO FIT YOUR FRAME. VOILÀ—INSTANT BOTANICAL.

materials

- Wooden picture frames
- Slip-joint pliers
- Dish soap
- Sandpaper
- Wood glue
- Concentrated artist's acrylic in colors to blend with frame
- Small artist's brush
- Floral image or color copy
- Chipboard
- Picture glass
- Brads
- Double-stick transfer tape (also called ATG or adhesive transfer gum tape)
- Brown kraft paper
- Craft knife
- Metal straightedge ruler
- Small eye hooks
- Lightweight picture wire

A

1 REMOVE ANY PICTURE WIRE, EYE HOOKS, OR PAPER FROM the back of the frame. Using the pliers, pull out the small brads holding the inside materials in place. Remove the backing board, the matted picture, and the glass from the frame. Clean any pieces of glass that can be reused and set aside. [photo A]

2 IF VERY GRIMY, CLEAN THE FRAMES WITH DISH SOAP AND a small amount of water, then sand lightly to remove more dirt and grime from the outside edges. If the frame is square and the corners are loose, they can be reglued and nailed as needed. [photo B]

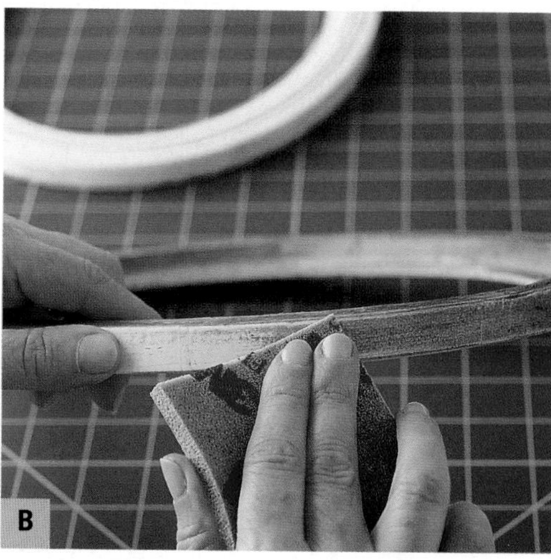

B

3 ANY VERY WORN SPOTS CAN BE TOUCHED UP WITH PAINT by mixing a color to match the frame. Carefully cover the chipped areas on the frame with 2 coats of the paint. Let dry between each coat and after the final coat. [photo C]

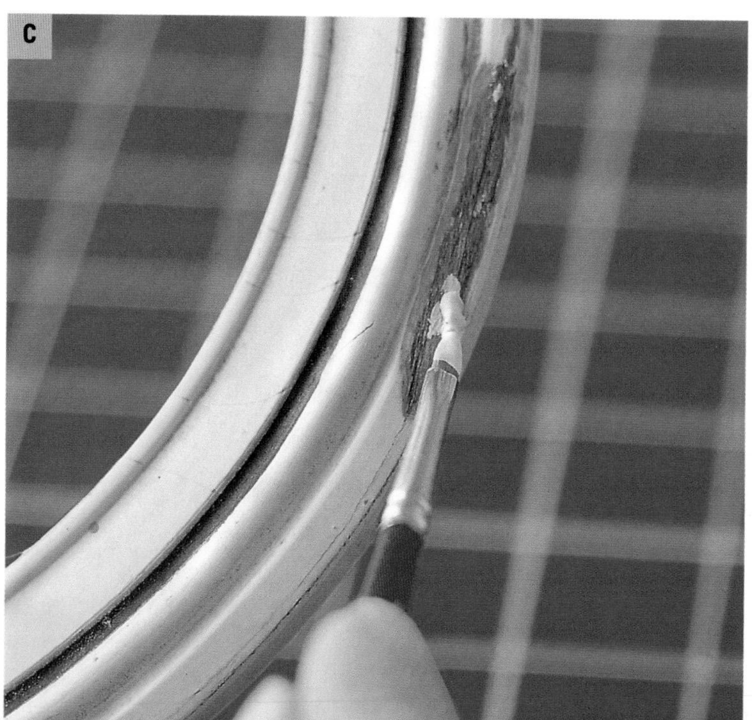

C

cleaning old prints and glass

To remove grease or grimy spots from an old print, use an art gum eraser or fresh white bread (roll into a ball like a gum eraser) and rub gently over the surface. Work over a piece of paper to catch the crumbs as they fall. Clean old glass with a little ammonia and water. Dry the glass with crumpled balls of newspaper. Remove old masking tape or stickers from glass by applying white vinegar directly to the surface, or use a cloth dampened with vinegar.

4 REASSEMBLE THE FRAME AND PICTURE, USING THE original material, or find a new image to fit the frame. For smaller frames look for art postcards or square-shaped greeting cards at museum stores, which usually have a great selection of botanical and other reproductions. If necessary, use a color copier to resize the image to fit your frame. Otherwise just use the original.

5 TO ADD A NEW PICTURE, TRIM OFF ANY EXCESS PAPER SO the image will fit the inside of the frame. Cut a new backing board out of the chipboard. To reassemble the frame, first place the cleaned glass in the frame, then the artwork, and last the new chipboard backing. [photo D]

E

6 HOLD THE BACKING IN PLACE BY INSERTING the brads into the frame using the slip-joint pliers, protecting the outside of the frame with a strip of chipboard or cardboard. [photo E]

7 ATTACH THE DOUBLE-STICK TRANSFER TAPE TO the back of the frame. Cut a piece of kraft paper 2 inches larger than the frame. Place the paper on the back of the frame, stretching the paper taut as you secure it to the tape. Trim about $\frac{1}{8}$ inch in from the edge, using the craft knife and a straightedge. [photo F]

F

arranging frames

The three different shapes of frames and the differences in scale play off of one another—each makes the other more interesting. I needed to find a new floral image to fit the square red frame that would complement the other images, but the unusual-looking botanical greeting card I wanted to use was too small for the frame. By making a color enlargement of the card on a copy machine, I was able to use the image I had found. Stacking the frames creates a pleasing arrangement on a narrow hallway wall and the red floral prints tie the different-sized frames together thematically. Hung on the green wall, which is the complementary color of red, the colors in the prints are set off strikingly.

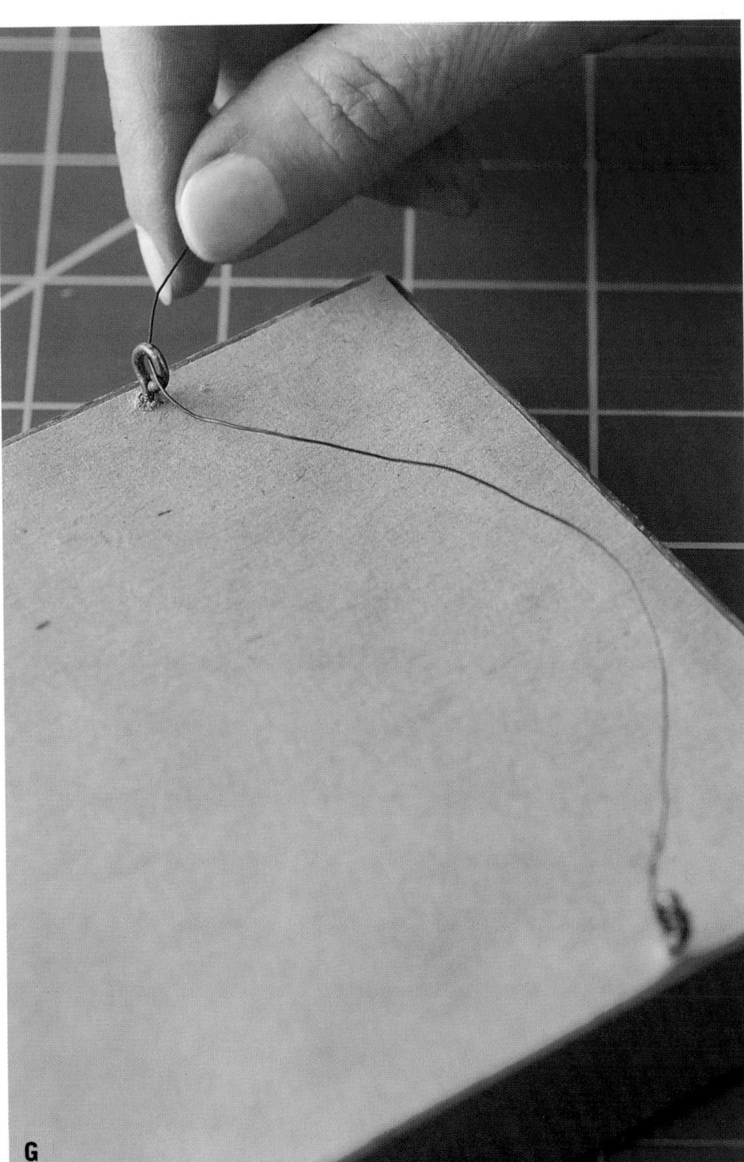

G

8 ADD THE EYE HOOKS A THIRD OF THE WAY DOWN THE SIDE of the frame and attach the picture wire to each hook by twisting each side back on itself. Allow some slack in the wire for hanging. [photo G]

Wicker Bed Tray

AT ONE TIME IT WAS A GREAT FANTASY OF MINE TO SPEND THE DAY IN BED HAVING BREAKFAST OFF JUST THIS TYPE OF TRAY, DRINKING TEA AND READING THE SUNDAY PAPERS. MY SISTER JANIS RESCUED THIS TRAY FROM THE BACK OF HER GARAGE, WHERE IT HAD LAIN FOR SEVERAL YEARS WITH ONLY DUST TO KEEP IT COMPANY. NEEDLESS TO SAY, THE TRAY WAS VERY SHABBY AND NEEDED A MAJOR OVERHAUL. I WANTED TO PAINT IT A BRIGHT COLOR WITH A GLOSSY FINISH, BUT DIDN'T WANT TO INVEST IN AN ENTIRE BRIGHT BLUE CAN OF PAINT THAT WOULD ONLY GROW DUSTY IN MY GARAGE. LUCKILY, I DISCOVERED SOME SIGN PAINTER'S LETTERING ENAMEL, WHICH IS USEFUL FOR SMALL PROJECTS BECAUSE IT'S AVAILABLE IN TWO DIFFERENT SMALL-SIZED CANS (FOUR OR EIGHT OUNCES) AND A LIMITED BUT FUN RANGE OF VIBRANT, HIGH-GLOSS COLORS.

materials

- Tray
- Scissors
- Fine-grade sandpaper or sponge
- Household paintbrush
- Acrylic primer
- Hot glue gun and glue stick
- Cotton clothesline
- Sign painter's lettering enamel
- ¼-inch-thick chipboard
- Spray adhesive
- Decorative paper
- Picture glass, if desired

1 CAREFULLY REMOVE THE TRIM HOLDING THE CARDBOARD insert in place. Set the pieces aside. Remove the old cardboard insert and set it aside to use as a template. [photo A]

2 CLIP ANY LOOSE ENDS OF THE OLD TRIM THAT ARE STICKING up. Remove or, if possible, reglue any of the loose spokes. [photo B]

3 SAND WITH THE FINE-GRADE SANDPAPER OR SPONGE TO remove any loose paint and smooth the surface. Undercoat the tray with the acrylic primer. [photo C]

4 TO COVER PROTRUDING NAILS AND REPLACE ANY DECORATIVE trim along the edge, use a length of cotton clothesline. It is soft and pliable enough to cover the uneven surface and can be painted. Use the hot glue gun to attach it along the top edge. [photo D]

A

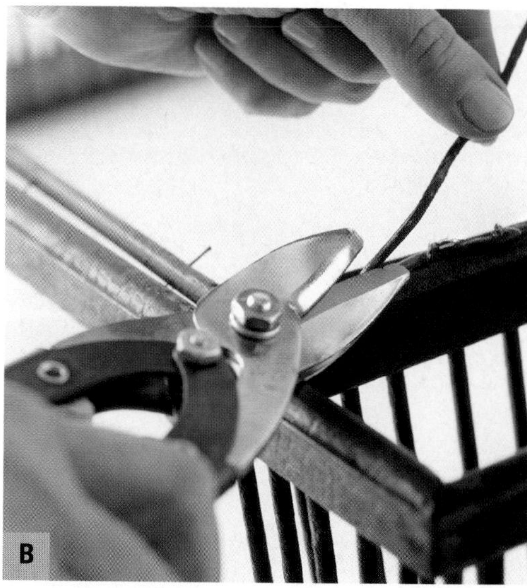

B

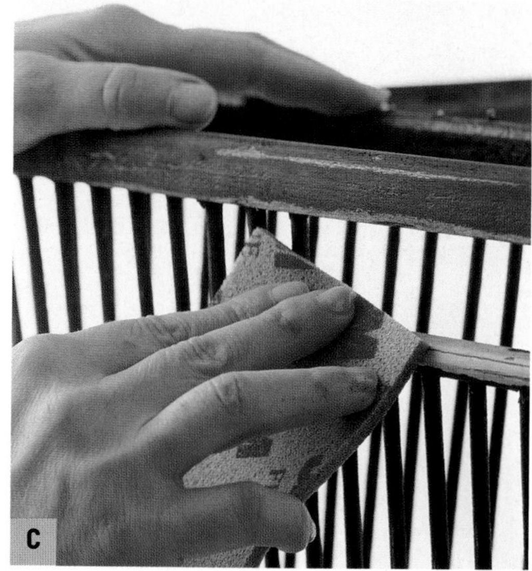

C

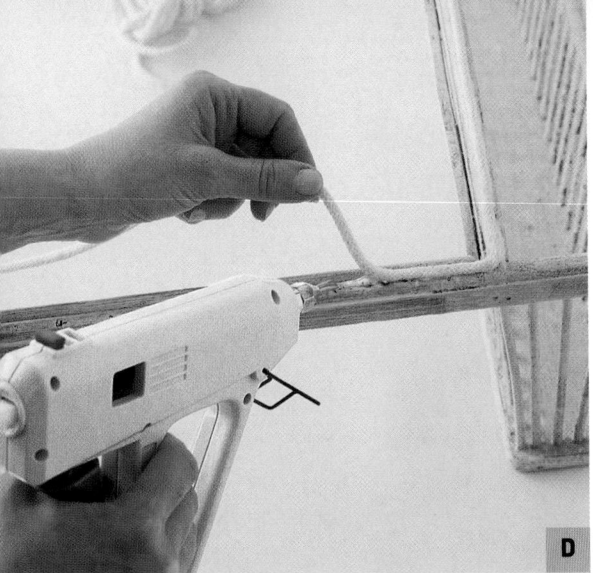
D

E

F

G

decorating the insert

If your bedroom is wallpapered, use some of the scraps to cover the insert or frame the insert with a mitered wallpaper border to match. Cut a motif, like a floral bouquet, out of paper or fabric and center it on a sheet of patterned paper. Use a scrap of antique fabric or lace mounted on the board. Vintage floral print hankies would also be fun; sew two or more together to make the right size. They can be glued to the board in the same way as the paper or they can be stretched over the board and taped on the underside of the board. Or do the same with cotton bandannas to match the colors in your bedroom.

5 WHEN THE GLUE IS COMPLETELY SET, APPLY 2 COATS OF THE sign painter's enamel. Let dry thoroughly between coats and after the final coat. [photo E]

6 REPLACE THE TRAY INSERT BY CUTTING A PIECE OF CHIPboard to size using the old insert as a pattern. Using spray adhesive, glue the decorative paper to one side of the board. [photo F]

7 ROLL THE PAPER OUT CAREFULLY ONTO THE BOARD, ALIGNing the pattern with the outside edges of the board. Trim the paper, leaving a 2-inch allowance on all sides of the board for turning. Fold the allowance to the inside and adhere to the underside of the board with spray adhesive. Fit the board in place in the tray and top with a piece of picture glass cut to the same size, if desired. Replace the trim on the tray to hold the top in place. [photo G]

Folding Screen

I DISCOVERED THIS FOLDING SCREEN AT A NEIGHBOR'S GARAGE SALE FOR ONLY $10. WITH THE PADDED FABRIC PANELS AND BEVELED MIRRORED INSERTS, THE SCREEN LOOKS MUCH MORE EXPENSIVE. THE MIRRORS ALSO GIVE THE SCREEN MORE SUBSTANCE, SO THAT IT SEEMS MORE LIKE A PIECE OF FURNITURE, AND THE ADDED WEIGHT GIVES IT SOME MUCH NEEDED STABILITY, AS IT WAS RATHER LIGHT IN WEIGHT BEFOREHAND. MANY THINGS CAN BE TURNED INTO SCREENS, SUCH AS DIFFERENT TYPES OF OLD SHUTTERS, SETS OF MULTIPANED GLASS DOORS, AND INTERESTING OLD WOOD DOORS OR WINDOW FRAMES, WITH OR WITHOUT THE GLASS. OTHER MATERIALS LIKE PAPER OR GLASS CAN ALSO BE USED TO DECORATE YOUR SCREEN. FABRIC AND PAPER CAN BE GLUED ONTO GLASS SURFACES, AND DEPENDING ON YOUR CHOICE CREATE AN OPAQUE OR TRANSLUCENT EFFECT—THINK OF JAPANESE SHOJI SCREENS. IF THE GLASS IS MISSING, FABRIC CAN BE HUNG IN ITS PLACE FROM NARROW CURTAIN RODS, OR USE THE FRAMES ALONE. JUST BE SURE TO ATTACH THE SECTIONS WITH DOUBLE-ACTION HINGES SO THE SCREEN CAN BEND IN EITHER DIRECTION.

materials

- Wood-frame folding screen
- Soft lead pencil
- Metal straightedge ruler
- Wood saw
- 1-inch-wide wood lattice
- Clear silicone glue or hot glue gun and glue stick
- Beveled mirrors
- Sandpaper
- Household paintbrush
- Acrylic primer
- Satin finish oil-based paint
- Foam-core board
- Scissors
- Cotton fabric
- Polyester batting
- T-pins
- Staple gun and staples
- Double-stick foam mounting tape
- Mirror adhesive
- Utility knife
- Cork sheeting
- Foam roller
- Eggshell finish water-based paint
- Floor adhesive

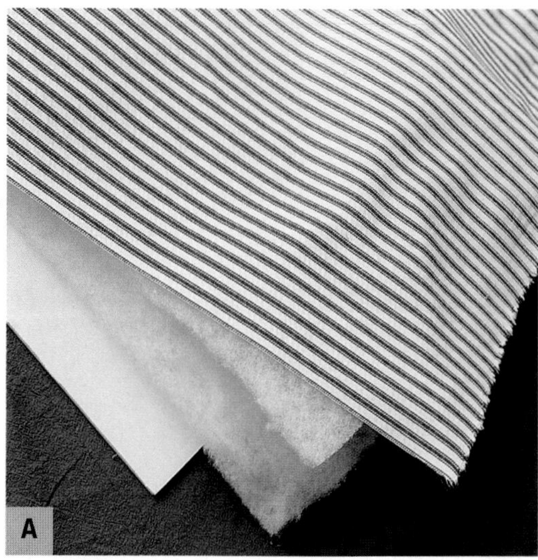
A

1 TO MAKE THE FRAMES FOR THE MIRRORS, USE THE PENCIL to mark a line across each of the panels 12 inches down from and parallel to the top edge. Measure the width of each panel along the marked line and, using a wood saw, cut a strip of lattice to fit across each of the panels. Measure each panel separately, as there might be small differences, and mark each corresponding length of lattice and panel for ease in assembling later. Lay the screen on a flat surface and use the hot glue gun to attach the strips of lattice to each panel following the pencil lines previously marked. The lattice strips should be positioned to fall above the line. Measure each of these framed openings carefully across all 4 sides for width and length, as they might be slightly uneven. Have 3 bevel-edge mirrors cut to fit each of the framed openings.

B

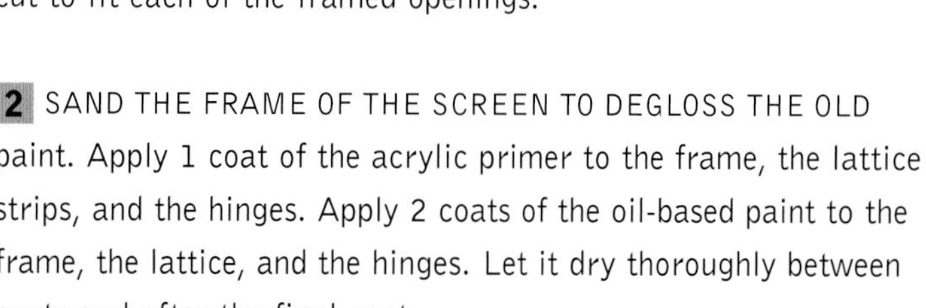

2 SAND THE FRAME OF THE SCREEN TO DEGLOSS THE OLD paint. Apply 1 coat of the acrylic primer to the frame, the lattice strips, and the hinges. Apply 2 coats of the oil-based paint to the frame, the lattice, and the hinges. Let it dry thoroughly between coats and after the final coat.

3 TO MAKE THE FABRIC-COVERED PADDED PANELS, MEASURE across the width and length of each panel on the screen below the lattice strip. Cut 3 pieces of foam-core board to fit each opening. Mark each corresponding piece of foam-core and panel. Cut a piece of ticking fabric to cover each board, allowing at least 2 inches on each side for wrapping and stretching the fabric around the board. Cut 2 pieces of batting, one the same size as the foam-core board and one 1 inch smaller all around. Center the 2 pieces of batting,

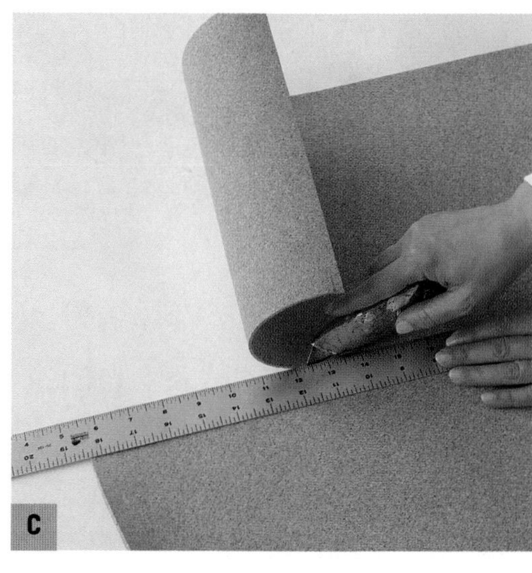
C

D

E

with the smaller piece underneath, on the foam-core and center the fabric on top. Insert a t-pin through the fabric and into the edge of the foam-core at the center of one long side. Align the grain of the fabric with the edge of the board, pin the fabric at each corner of the same side, pulling the fabric taut between pins. Wrap the excess fabric to the back of the board, pulling firmly, and staple in place. Complete one side at a time, starting in the center and working out toward the corners. Fold in the excess fabric at the corners and staple in place. [photo A]

4 LAY THE SCREEN FLAT WITH THE LATTICE side up. Secure the double-stick foam tape to each screen panel close to the edges in each of the openings for the padded fabric panels. Position the padded panels in each screen opening and press into place. Apply the mirror adhesive to the backs of the mirrors and glue the mirrors in place in the framed openings on top of each screen panel. [photo B]

5 TO MAKE CORK-COVERED PANELS ON THE OPPOSITE SIDE OF the screen, measure each long panel as directed above. Using the straightedge and a utility knife, cut a length of cork to fit each space. Using the roller, paint the lengths of cork with water-based paint. When dry, glue the cork in place. [photos C, D, and E]

Oval Velvet Bench

OLD PIANO BENCHES AND OTHER SMALL BENCHES TURN UP WITH SURPRISING REGULARITY AT THRIFT STORES. THE OVAL-SHAPED SEAT AND ELEGANT TAPERED LEGS GIVE THIS PIANO BENCH A DELICATE AND REFINED AIR. SIMPLE WHITE PAINT AND THE LUXURIOUS SKY-BLUE VELVET CREATE A REFRESHING COMBINATION THAT FURTHER ENHANCES THE BENCH'S CHARMING DETAILS. IF THE BENCH YOU COME ACROSS IS OF THE MORE FAMILIAR STURDY, RECTANGULAR SHAPE, DON'T DESPAIR. THESE MORE MODERN-LOOKING BENCHES USUALLY HAVE LESS DETAIL AND THEREFORE CAN CARRY A MUCH BOLDER FABRIC, SUCH AS A LARGE-SCALE VINTAGE FLORAL PRINT OR A WIDE AWNING STRIPE.

BOVARY
GUSTAVE FLAUBERT

materials

Bench
Screwdriver
Black permanent marker
Pliers
Scissors
1-inch-thick foam
Polyester batting
Staple gun and staples
Ruler
Soft lead pencil
Upholstery fabric
Putty knife
Wood putty
Sandpaper
Household paintbrush
Acrylic primer
Eggshell finish water-based paint

1 TAKE THE BENCH APART BY TURNING IT UPSIDE DOWN, locating the screw holes, and unscrewing the top from the base. Set the screws aside. Mark the underside of both the frame and the base with black permanent marker to indicate which way the frame sits in the base. Mark each piece with an X to indicate the sides that go together. After the seat is off, remove the curved backrest if there is one, reserving it for possible use in a future project. [photo A]

2 REMOVE THE SCREWS HOLDING THE PADDED SEAT TO THE wooden rim and set the screws aside, carefully marking which screws are used where. Again, mark the corresponding sides on the underside of both seat and frame. [photo B]

A

B

C

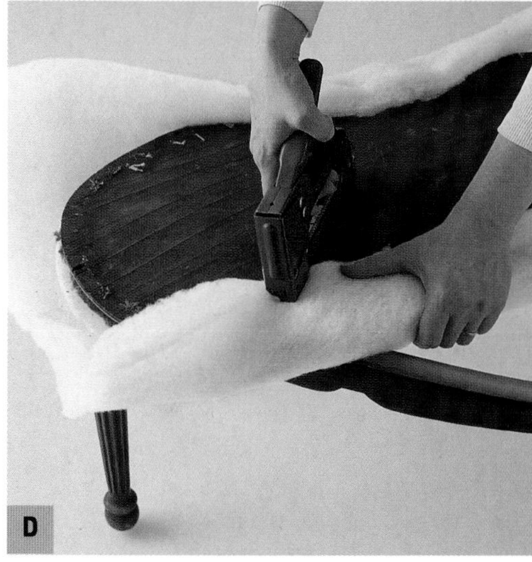
D

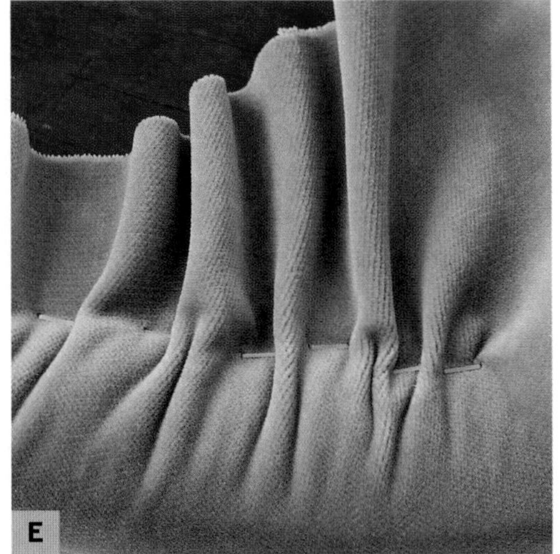

E

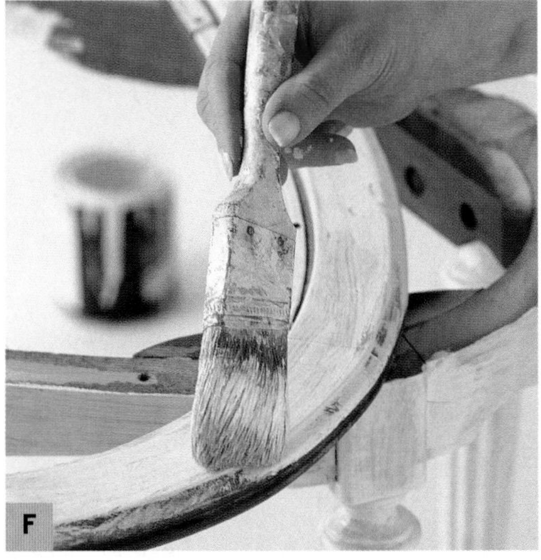

F

small parts

Zip-lock bags or small screw-top jars are great for storing and organizing small parts like screws that you need to use later. Label the outside of the bag or container so there is no confusion when you are putting things back together.

3 WITH THE PLIERS AND SCREWDRIVER, REMOVE THE staples or tacks holding the seat cover in place and remove the old cover. Using the screwdriver, lift up the edge of the staple and pull the loosened staple out with the pliers. Set the old cover aside to use as a pattern. [photo C]

4 USING THE WOODEN OVAL BASE AS A PATTERN, CUT A PIECE of foam to fit the base. Cut out new padding from the polyester batting, again using the base as a pattern, allowing 4 inches extra all around for wrapping around the base. Wrap the batting around the base and staple in place, stretching it tightly over the wooden base as you go. Start by stapling the batting to the base with one staple in the middle of each of the opposite long sides, then continue to staple on either side of the centers, alternating from side to side, pulling the batting tight. After continuing to staple the batting to the base for a few more inches on either long side, start stapling the batting to the shorter sides of the oval, starting again in the middle of either opposite end. Ease in the fullness on the curves as you continue around the oval. After you have completed stapling the batting in place, it can be trimmed close to the staples if desired. [photo D]

5 USING THE OLD COVER AS A PATTERN, CUT A NEW ONE OUT of the upholstery fabric, again adding 4 to 5 inches extra all around. Staple in place over the batting in exactly the same fashion as above and trim the fabric when finished, if desired. [photo E]

6 USING A PUTTY KNIFE, FILL THE HOLES IN THE FRAME where the curved back piece was attached with wood putty, if necessary. Let dry and sand lightly. Lightly sand the whole frame to help the paint adhere better and smooth out any rough spots.

7 APPLY 1 COAT OF THE ACRYLIC PRIMER TO THE FRAME. SAND lightly again and apply 2 coats of water-based paint. Let dry thoroughly between coats and after the final coat. [photo F]

8 PLACE THE PADDED SEAT IN THE OVAL FRAME AND SCREW in place, using the original screws. Attach the seat to the frame with the remaining screws, carefully making holes in the fabric if necessary so that the screws connect to the wooden base below.

Basic Techniques

While a project might require specific techniques and tools, there are two rules of thumb to remember before tackling any of them.

Use the correct tools for the job; it will make your life easier. For the most part you don't have to buy expensive specialized tools to do the projects in this book, though it's worth investing in a few good-quality paintbrushes that won't lose their bristles. I also recommend buying an orbital sander. Porter and Cable makes a good one that is very lightweight and easy to maneuver. It will save you hours of preparation time, especially if you are planning to do two or more furniture makeovers.

Prepare the surface carefully for the best results. Perfectly good results can be achieved by simply painting over the original finish if it is prepared first—and preparing the surface will also save you time. Sand any previously painted surface using sandpaper or the power sander to provide a smooth, nonglossy surface (make sure to wear a mask). Alternatively, if the finish or paint is too thick, badly cracked, sticky, or uneven, it can be removed with a nontoxic paint remover or furniture refinisher, following the directions on the container. If you decide to remove the old paint or finish entirely, you should sand the piece lightly when you are done. Before proceeding to paint or refinish, remove any sanding dust with a soft rag.

TOOLS

The Basic Tool Kit

Flat-head and Phillips screwdrivers, hammer, pliers, wire cutters, adjustable wrench, putty knife, rotary drill, orbital sander, wood saw, sharp craft knife, single edge razor blades, staple gun, retractable tape measure, metal-edge ruler, masking tape, lead pencil, permanent marker, wood and craft glue.

The Basic Sewing Kit

Sharp scissors, iron, transparent gridded ruler, cloth tape measure, lead pencil, straight pins, t-pins, hand-sewing needles, white, black, and beige cotton thread.

The Basic Paint Kit

Large and small household paintbrushes, square- and round-tip artist's brushes, combing tool, painter's tape, conte pencil, cheesecloth, soft cotton rags (old white cotton T-shirts make the best rags).

Two Useful Tools for Small Spaces

For cleaning, refinishing, and other tasks, use an old toothbrush and a thin pointed implement like a dental pick (often available at flea markets). Use them for narrow crevices and tight corners.

CLEANING

Mild Stains and Dirt

Wash mildly soiled furniture or other objects with a soft, clean rag and warm water to which a small amount of a mild dishwashing detergent (like Ivory) has been added. Do not soak furniture or let the water set on it. Wipe dry with clean rags or paper towels.

Light Rust

Clean metal by applying naval jelly to the surface. Leave on for 5 to 10 minutes. Rinse off with water. Repeat if any rust remains. You can also rub the surface lightly with a fine-grade steel wool pad over the naval jelly. Alternatively, for very light rust, rub the surface with a fine-grade steel wool pad dipped in vegetable oil. Use this only on steel or iron. Do not use it on aluminum or chrome.

Light Stains on Marble

Rub light stains with toothpaste and a clean rag. Rinse thoroughly with water. Dry with a clean rag. Use a small amount of toothpaste

and an old toothbrush to give a quick polish to small metal fittings like knobs and hinges. Rinse thoroughly.

Paper Stuck to Wood

Remove a piece of paper by pouring enough warm lightweight oil on the surface to saturate the paper. Let stand. Rub lightly with a very fine steel wool pad. Apply more warm oil and rub again. Wipe the surface with the oil, and then dry with a clean cloth.

Grease and Dirt Spots on Prints

To remove marks on a vintage print, use an art gum eraser or fresh white bread (roll it into a ball like a gum eraser) and rub gently over the surface of the print.

Streaks and Dust on Glass

Clean glass by filling a spray bottle with water to which you have added a small amount of ammonia. Spray solution on the surface. Dry and polish the glass with newspaper.

Masking Tape and Stickers on Glass

Remove old masking tape or stickers with a cloth dampened with white vinegar. Nail polish remover, turpentine, and prewash spray can also be effective in loosening the glue on stickers.

Rust Stains on Fabric

Remove rust stains with lemon juice and salt. Apply directly to the stain and let it sit for a few minutes. Stretch the fabric over the top of any heat-resistant (metal or tempered glass) bowl, and pour boiling water through the fabric until the stain is out.

REPAIRING

Tighten Square-Sided or Rectangular Joints

Use a shim for square-sided (or rectangular) joints. This works especially well for the stretchers that fit in the legs of chairs and tables, which frequently become loose through hard use. Make a shim —it can be of even thickness or slightly tapered—out of a small scrap of wood (hardwood is best), but it should be as wide as the hole. Apply glue to the hole and drive the shim in place. Apply more glue and reassemble the joint. Wipe any excess off with a damp cloth.

Tighten Square or Round Joints

Use cloth strips for square or round joints. Cut some cloth (from an old sheet or shirt) into strips. The strips should be narrower than the end of the part you're inserting. Place the strips over the end of the part in the form of an X. Trim the strips on the sides so they are about two-thirds of the depth of the joint—the cloth will stretch when the pieces are joined. Apply glue and reassemble the joint. Trim any cloth protruding after the joint is assembled with a razor blade, and wipe any excess glue off with a damp cloth.

Fill in Small Cracks, Surface Dents, Holes, and Other Surface Blemishes

Working on a clean surface, apply a lightweight spackling paste, like UGI 222 Lite or wood putty, over any chips, cracks, or other dents. Deeper holes might need more than one application of the paste. Push the paste down into the cracks with the putty knife. Draw a damp knife across the surface, smoothing the excess paste as you go. Let the putty dry until hard. The paste type of filler does not usually require sanding, but if necessary, sand the surface lightly with fine-grade sandpaper.

Wire a New Lamp or Rewire an Old One

The easiest and fastest way is to use a self-clamping lamp socket. Use it with a prewired cord set (where the plug is already attached to the lamp cord) and you will be done in a flash. The cord sets can be found in solid colors like ivory, white, or brown, or my favorites: a transparent covering with silver-colored wires or a gold-tinted transparent covering with copper-colored wires. Pick the one that best matches your lamp. Lamps should always be rewired if the cord is old and brittle or the covering is cracked, cut, ripped, or frayed. The sockets will need to be replaced only if the switch is not working or if the terminals (the screws where the wires are attached) are corroded. If in doubt, I suggest you replace both the socket and the wiring, as the costs are minimal.

Make a New Cushion Pad

Cut 2 pieces of cotton muslin or old cotton sheeting the same size as the cushion cover. Cut 2 pieces of polyester batting or one piece each of polyester and cotton batting slightly smaller than the cushion cover. Center the 2 pieces of batting—I used one of each of polyester and cotton batting—on one piece of fabric and center the second fabric piece on top. Machine stitch together, enclosing the batting in the fabric covering. Insert into the cushion cover and plump.

REFINISHING

Remove Old Paint or Multiple Finishes from Wood or Metal Furniture

A paint remover such as Zip-Strip is a fast alternative to sanding. Work outside where possible or in a well-ventilated space. Wear rubber gloves and a protective mask. Apply the remover liberally with an old paintbrush. Let the remover stand for 15 to 20 minutes until finish is softened and the surface appears crinkly. Don't let the remover dry out. Remove the loosened paint or finish by scraping with a rounded-edged putty knife, wiping it on old newspaper from time to time. Wipe off as much of the remaining finish as possible using crumpled paper towels. Dip a pad of fine-grade steel wool in remover and scrub the surface for a final cleaning. Wipe dry with a clean rag.

Remove Old Varnish, Lacquer, and Shellac Finishes

A furniture refinisher like Minwax Antique Furniture Refinisher dissolves old finishes in minutes and is less messy than standard paint removers. Wearing rubber gloves and a protective mask, pour a small amount of the refinisher into a glass or metal container. Dip a pad of fine-grade steel wool in the refinisher, squeezing out the excess, and rub on the surface along the grain of the wood until the finish is dissolved. Wipe off occasionally with a clean paper towel or rag. Repeat as needed. When finish is completely gone, go back over the surface with a pad of clean steel wool dipped in clean refinisher. Dry by wiping with a clean rag.

Varnish Stripped and Unpainted Wood Surfaces

A protective, penetrating oil finish (like Formby's Tung Oil Finish in low gloss) will give you a natural, hand-rubbed classic look. This type of finish penetrates the wood and dries clear, allowing the natural beauty of the wood to come through. Pour a small amount of the tung oil on a soft rag and rub into the wood. Allow it to dry and buff it with a fine-grade steel wool pad. Wipe it down with a clean rag and repeat until you have achieved the desired finish. Let dry completely.

Apply Water-Based Stains on Unfinished or Stripped Wood Surfaces

If you don't want to paint your wood piece, you can add color or a complementary wood tone by staining. With a small paintbrush, apply the water-based stain liberally over the surface, working on a small area at a time. Allow the stain to penetrate the surface no longer than three to five minutes. While the stain is still wet, use a clean rag or a piece of cheesecloth to wipe off the excess, working in the direction of the wood grain. Let dry and repeat again, if desired.

PAINTING

Prepare the Wood Before Painting

Sand the piece with a power sander or by hand with sandpaper; remove the dust with a rag or a brush and wipe down with a damp paper towel. Let dry thoroughly.

Prime the Wood Before Painting

If you need to prime the surface I recommend using an acrylic primer, which adheres well to a variety of surfaces, is quick drying, and cleans up with water. Apply one coat and let it dry thoroughly. Sand lightly and remove dust before proceeding.

Paint with Water-Based Paints

Look for either a satin finish paint (which when dry has a slight sheen) or an eggshell finish paint (which when dry has a matte finish). Two coats of paint are best, but sometimes one will do. Let the first coat dry, sand lightly and remove dust before applying the second coat. Let piece dry thoroughly before using.

Paint with Oil-Based Paint

These paints are much messier and smellier to work with, but sometimes they're a good choice for pieces that have previously been painted with an oil-based paint. The new paint will adhere better and you don't have to strip off all of the old paint before applying the new coat. Oil-based paint also has a different surface texture than water-based paint; it's not dry like water-based paint and has a lovely, dull sheen well worth the extra work.

Age New Paint

New paint can be given a vintage look by applying a transparent glaze to the surface after the paint has dried. Add a small amount of raw umber paint to some water or glaze medium and lightly brush this mixture onto the painted item. If it still looks too new once the glaze dries, repeat or try lightly washing the piece with water.

resources

The Lamp Shop
PO Box 3606
Concord, NH 03302-3606
(603) 244-1603
fax (603) 224-6677
lampshop@juno.com
www.lampshop.com
Good source for mail-order lamp-shade crafting supplies, materials, and other small shade-related lamp parts. They are very helpful on the phone and also carry a useful series of instructional booklets for making different types of lamp shades.

Just Shades
21 Spring St.
New York, NY 10012
(212) 966-2757
fax (212) 334-6129
They have a very extensive selection of paper and cloth lamp shades at the store and will also make custom shades. If you go in person, be sure to bring your lamp.

Grand Brass Lamp Parts
221 Grand Street
New York, NY 10013
(212) 226-2567
(800) 645-9548
www.grandbrass.com
A very large section of new and replacement lamp parts. They will rewire old lamps or make lamps out of an old wooden column or vintage vase.

Dykes Lumber Company (main yard and general offices)
1899 Park Ave.
Weehawken, NJ 07087
(201) 867-0391
fax (201) 867-1674
A wide range of specialty moldings and other building materials. They have a catalog of moldings and trims, as well as stores in New York and New Jersey.

B&J Fabrics
263 W. 40th St.
New York, NY 10018
(212) 764-3355

Rosen & Chadick
246 W. 40th St.
New York, NY 10018
(212) 869-0136
Both of these fabric stores have a large selection of home furnishing fabrics and designer fabrics. Both welcome mail-order business.

Waverly
(800) 423-5881
www.waverly.com
They make all the basics and more—a wonderful selection of checks, stripes, ticking, and florals at reasonable prices. As their fabrics are available in many national outlets, this is a good basic choice for a home furnishings project. Call for stores nearest you or store listings.

Rogers & Goffigon Ltd.
41 Chestnut St.
Greenwich, CT 06830
To the trade only—you may be able to buy fabric from them through a decorator. They make some of the most innovative, luxurious, and stunningly beautiful fabrics. Use this resource for a special piece or project, as the fabrics are quite expensive.

Clotilde
Box 3000
Louisiana, MO 63335
(800) 772-2891
www.clotilde.com
A comprehensive mail-order catalog for sewing notions and supplies.

Viking Sewing Machines, Inc.
31000 Viking Parkway
Westlake, OH 44145
(440) 808-6550
(800) 358-0001
www.husqvarnaviking.com
An excellent sewing machine for basic home and specialty sewing. Available with many specialized accessories to make your sewing faster, easier, and more professional. They have outlets across the country.

Plaid
PO Box 7600
Norcross, GA 30091
(800) 842-4197
www.plaidonline.com
Manufacturer of Folk Art concentrated artist's pigment acrylic paint. The perfect paint for many small projects, it is available in handy 2-ounce containers, as well as a large range of pure, true acrylic colors that are completely intermixable with each other and can be used to tint white and other colors. They also offer brushes and other painting supplies and kits.

Pearl Paint
308 Canal St.
New York, NY 10013
(212) 431-7932
(800) 221-6845 ext. 2297
Discount art and craft supplies—one of the largest sources. Visit one of their many stores or call for a mail-order catalog.

New York Central Art Supply
62 Third Ave.
New York, NY 10003
(212) 477-0400
To order: (800) 950-6111
fax (212) 475-2513
www.nycentralart.com
Fine art paper specialists with a very extensive selection of imported and domestic papers, bookbinding supplies, and some papermaking supplies. Call for mail-order catalog.

A SPECIAL THANKS TO SOME OF MY LOCAL SHOPS:

Cat House Antiques
136 Bruceville Rd.
High Falls, NY 12440
(914) 687-0457
Colorful 1930s to 1950s kitchenware, furniture, and collectibles.

Linger Corner Gift Company
PO Box 367
8 Second St.
High Falls, NY 12440
(914) 687-7907
Vintage and new home accessories and special gifts.

Saultana Upholstered Furniture
512 Lem Boice Lane
Kingston, NY 12401
(914) 336-6606
Custom upholstery.

SOME USEFUL REFERENCE BOOKS:

Kevin McCloud's Complete Book of Paint and Decorative Techniques
Simon & Schuster, New York
A good comprehensive technique book with excellent information on using and mixing colors.

Laura Ashley Complete Guide to Home Decorating
Harmony Books, New York
Just what it says—covers everything from walls to lamp shades.

Simply Upholstery
Sunset Books, Menlo Park, CA
An excellent book for beginners, it explains everything from tools to techniques and takes you step by step through the upholstery process.

Upholstery Basics (Singer Sewing Reference Library)
Creative Publishing International, Minnetonka, MN
Another good book, very thorough, with full-color photographs.

Home Decorating Basics
by Pamela J. Hastings
Sterling Publishing Co., New York
A good basic book for beginners—covers all the basics on sewing projects for your home.

Simply Slipcovers
Sunset Books, Menlo Park, CA
Useful book, covering both the basics and designer details, with directions for 20 different slipcover projects.

The Lamp Shade Book: 80 Traditional & Innovative Projects to Create Exciting Lighting Effects
by Dawn Cusick
Lark Books, Asheville, NC
A good book for beginners, with easy-to-follow basic lamp-shade instructions and a large variety of innovative lamp-shade projects.

Lampshades (Home Living Workbook)
by Katrin Cargill
Clarkson Potter, New York
A very pretty and useful book showing a large variety of the more traditional types of fabric and paper lamp shades. Many charming details and easy-to-follow instructions.

Making Great Lamps: 50 Illuminating Projects, Techniques & Ideas
by Deborah Morgenthal
Lark Books, Asheville, NC
A useful book with very good basic step-by-step instructions and interesting projects for untraditional lamps, many made with unusual materials.

Frame It Yourself: Matting & Framing Step-by-Step
Creative Publishing International, Minnetonka, MN
This 64-page paperback is small but very comprehensive, covering all the basics and more with clear step-by-step photos and instructions.

index